What people are
Leaving Hom

CH01019324

"As one who has gone through the struggle of 'leaving homosexuality' personally, all I can say is, 'Where was this book 27 years ago?' What a wonderful resource for those who find themselves in the midst of that struggle. Written with great compassion, this book exudes the convicting truth of Christ and clearly conveys realistic expectations facing those who struggle. *Leaving Homosexuality* is a beacon of hope bathed in the love of Jesus Christ."

Dennis Jernigan, author, song writer,
recording artist (Shepherd's Heart Music)

"The true Church has been consistent with their stand against homosexuality but less faithful in providing an adequate answer for those who struggle with same-sex attractions. *Leaving Homosexuality* makes a major contribution in correcting this deficiency and offers hope to those who long for a righteous relationship with their heavenly Father."

Dr. Neil T. Anderson, founder and president emeritus,
Freedom in Christ Ministries

"This moving account of Alan's personal journey out of homosexuality offers solid answers and real hope to men and women struggling with same-sex attraction. This book is a must-read for those searching for an honest, biblically based account of how freedom from homosexuality can occur in the body of Christ!"

Bill Maier, psychologist in residence,
Focus on the Family

"In a world of sexual confusion this book is a compass that points the way to freedom with compassion and clarity. I applaud Alan for having the courage and transparency to write it. I truly believe it is a book for our time and for every person dealing with homosexuality."

Jimmy Evans, president and founder,
MarriageToday

"Alan supports the truth that 'Yes you can!' Change is possible. Leaving homosexuality is possible. If anyone can speak honestly and lovingly and hopefully, it is Alan Chambers."

Dr. Nancy Heche Schoeberl,
author of *The Truth Comes Out*

"As a psychiatrist, I have lovingly counseled hundreds of homosexual clients over the past 34 years for a wide variety of conditions. Some wanted to only work on their depression and didn't want to even discuss their sexual orientation. Others were more concerned with their attractions and how to handle them. Is change possible? they wondered. I was able to assure them that, yes, change is not only possible but predictable with the right kinds of therapy to repair issues from their past. That is why I am very pleased with Alan Chamber's book *Leaving Homosexuality.* Why shouldn't a homosexual who chooses to change be free to do so? And now, for those who do choose to pursue change, *Leaving Homosexuality* gives the stepping-stones necessary. I highly recommend it."

Paul Meier, MD, author and founder of
Meier Clinics (www.meierclinics.org)

"A personal and powerful story coupled with practical insight that will not only help those looking to leave homosexuality, but will also serve as a wonderful resource for those in the church. I believe this book will open hearts as well as educate and equip people in the body of Christ that need to provide an authentic and healing community to those desiring to be free of same-sex attractions."

Dale Evrist, pastor, New Song Christian Fellowship,
and author of *The Mighty Hand of God*

"This is the first book I've read that effectively portrays the real-life struggle of countless people both within and outside the body of Christ who are struggling with same-sex attraction. Alan Chambers offers hope with his in-depth look at Jesus' forgiveness, mercy, compassion, and transforming power over sin. Alan's stories will break your heart, convict your conscience, and hopefully inspire today's church to reexamine its messages on this complex issue."

Miles McPherson, Sr. pastor, The Rock Church,
former NFL player for Chargers and Rams

Leaving Homosexuality

Alan Chambers

HARVEST HOUSE PUBLISHERS

EUGENE, OREGON

LEAVING HOMOSEXUALITY
Copyright © 2009 by Alan Chambers
Published by Harvest House Publishers
Eugene, Oregon 97402
www.harvesthousepublishers.com

Library of Congress Cataloging-in-Publication Data
   Chambers, Alan.
   Leaving homosexuality / Alan Chambers.
     p. cm.
   ISBN 978-0-7369-2610-2 (pbk.)
   1. Homosexuality—Religious aspects—Christianity. 2. Church work with gays. I. Title.
   BR115.H6C425 2009
   261.8'35766—dc22

                2009002478

To my dad, Robert Chambers.
Without you I wouldn't be the
husband, father, and man I am today.
I miss you every day, Dad,
but you still spur me on to greatness!

Acknowledgments

My sincere thanks goes to everyone who aided me in the writing of this book.

First and foremost, I'm grateful to my Lord and Savior, Jesus Christ, for saving me, sustaining me, and giving me a testimony to share.

My life today wouldn't be complete without my Leslie. She is and always will be the best part of my life on Earth.

Isaac and Molly, I treasure you both and am overwhelmed with love and gratefulness every day because I get to be your dad. I'm so glad God chose you to be our kids!

I'm so thankful for the rescue team Jesus sent to aid me in my journey toward wholeness—the people of Discovery Church (1992–1995), including my brother and sister-in-law, Fred and Kim Chambers, my friends Kirk Bane, David and Caron Loveless, Tom, Bud, and Neal. I wouldn't be here if not for all of you!

I also appreciate the family I found at Exchange Ministries. When I desperately needed friends to stick as close as brothers during the intense early battles that threatened my pursuit of freedom, you were here for me. Mike, Rick, Gary, Greg, John, and the rest of you—thanks!

My team at Exodus International is great. I'm especially grateful for the help of Leya Macchi, who transcribed hours of notes and talks; my friend and assistant, Melissa, for helping me find notes and articles I'd lost; Yvette Schneider and Mike Goeke, for adding their wisdom to this book. Exodus is a success because of the team God has assembled.

And to my friend and editor, Nick Harrison. Man, you are the best. Thanks for being so good and patient and wise.

Contents

Part 1

Starting Here, Starting Now

Part 2

Moving into Wholeness

Part 3

Special Considerations

Part 4

Staying the Course

Another Option

Do you remember when you first realized you were same-sex attracted? If you're like most of us, you were probably very young. You knew there was something different about you, but for a long time you couldn't figure out what it was. And then, perhaps sometime near puberty or shortly thereafter, the lightbulb came on.

You had heard the word "homosexual" before. You may even have been called one of the many pejoratives that set you apart from your peers. You were a "queer," "sissy," "fag," "dyke," or some other negative name. And suddenly you knew it was true. You were sexually drawn to your own gender and had little or zero attraction to the opposite sex.

How on earth did *that* happen? How could it be? And why *you*?

Every gay-identified person on the planet has asked that question many times over. Usually the answers are very unsatisfactory, if any come at all.

After a while you finally realize it really didn't matter if you were born this way or if your parents somehow messed up or if something else happened. The result was still the same. Your life was set apart in a way that would affect not just your sexuality but your entire being. And with that realization came perhaps the biggest question of all: What were you going to do about it?

Was there anything you *could* do about it? Is there anything you can do now?

On the following pages, you'll find an answer you may not have considered. This book is essentially an invitation to a new life in which your sexual attractions are no longer the defining aspect of who you are. It's an invitation to a life presently enjoyed by many men and women who were dissatisfied with their lives being defined by their sexual attractions.

Most of us who have accepted this invitation didn't realize for a long time that there was another option for us. We assumed, as most gay men and women do, that because we have same-sex attractions, the only way to a satisfactory life is to embrace those attractions, act on them, and essentially build a life around them.

But for many of us, the sad truth was that accepting our attractions and acting on them was a dead-end street leading to profound despair. Maybe that's where you are now. Or are you perhaps still enthralled with the gay life? If your experience is like ours, I'm guessing that one day you'll realize there *has* to be a better life for you.

No matter where you are in the continuum of homosexual discovery, please consider the invitation of this book seriously. My prayer is that either now or in the near future you'll want to join those of us who have decided against building a life based on sexual attraction and, instead, decided to follow the One whose 2000-year-old invitation still stands. Jesus Christ said, "Come to me, all you who are weary and burdened, and I will give you rest" (Matthew 11:28).

Part 1

Starting Here, Starting Now

1

A Life-changing Choice

I didn't choose to be gay, and I'm pretty sure you didn't either. My friend and mentor Sy Rogers says it best: "Out of life's great big buffet, I didn't choose to feel gay."

Seriously, I have never met anyone with same-sex attractions who would say he or she had a choice when it came to their feelings.

Sadly, most voices in the debate over whether or not one chooses to be gay or can choose to overcome being gay have completely overlooked the complexity of the issue. They've tried to whittle same-sex attractions down to a rigid conclusion that supports their side of the debate. On the conservative side we hear the claim that homosexuality is a choice. One can *choose* to be a homosexual or a heterosexual. On the other, more liberal side, we hear that there is no choice at all when it comes to homosexual behavior. It's an inborn trait.

The truth is that both are somewhat right and somewhat wrong. Though we didn't choose our homosexual attractions, *we do have a choice* as to what we do with them. I didn't choose my homosexual feelings, but when I was old enough to choose what to do with those feelings, I opted to accept and act on them. I chose to look at gay pornography, to go to gay bars, and to have sexual relations with other men. I could have chosen differently, but I didn't. No one forced me to do any of those things. They were my decisions.

As is often the case, eventually my choices led to a sexual addiction...and when a person's choice becomes an addiction, the ability to choose becomes severely limited. But even then there remained one choice I could make: whether to seek help or allow myself to become more entrenched in a life that was destroying me.

> You have a choice as to what the rest of your life is going to look like.

I chose to get help.

Although for a while I continued to choose to give in to my addiction, I also submitted to the authority of others who were committed to helping me break free of what was holding me captive. Ultimately, my choice to seek help was what led to my freedom.

Note: Don't let someone tell you that you don't have options. You *do.* If you're young and *thinking* about experimenting with same-sex attractions or if you're sexually active—and even if you've been sexually active for years—you have a choice as to what the rest of your life is going to look like. And your destiny will be a result of the choices you make along the way.

My passion for writing this book is to help you make a choice that will give you the best life possible. I want to share the joy and freedom I have found so you'll know you have another option for handling sexual attractions.

Beginning the Journey

The first and most important choice we make is one that's not unique to homosexuality. In fact, it's a decision everyone—straights and gays alike—must make. It's accepting God's forgiveness and beginning a new life as His child. That happens by entering into a personal relationship with His Son, Jesus Christ. Essentially, this is how a person becomes a Christian.

Most people at least know *about* Jesus, but general knowledge is not what I'm talking about. I'm referring to knowing Him as He desires to be known. He wants to be known as the one who has loved you since before you were born. Who knew everything about you as you were growing up...even as your same-sex attractions were being formed. He knew you then, and He knows you now. He knows your every heartache and your every joy.

The way we enter into this kind of knowing and believing is through a commitment to Him, expressed in a prayer inviting Jesus Christ to be the Lord of our lives. It happens by putting our *faith* in Christ. By simply believing. This is a decisive act on our part. We *decide* to put our hope and trust in Him.

God doesn't make it hard to enter into a relationship with Him. Even a child can do it. In fact, children do it best. Jesus made the way simple. You only have to acknowledge and confess Him as Lord of your life.

It's that easy.

We complicate it sometimes. And, to be honest, many men and women who struggle with same-sex attraction have a distorted and untrusting image of what it means to become or be a Christian. The misguided actions of some Christians may be stumbling blocks to some who desire to be set free. When they think of Christianity, all they see are the angry faces of protestors who rail against sexual sins to the exclusion of all other sins.

Maybe this isn't my place, but I want to apologize on behalf of those Christians who say the wrong thing at the wrong time to hurting, broken, and seeking people. To tell someone—especially one who doesn't know Christ—that they need to have heterosexual feelings in order to be a Christian is simply wrong. How reckless, un-Christlike, and flat-out ridiculous.

In my own case, I became a Christian prior to puberty and the development of any sexual feelings. Imagine my surprise (and disappointment) when I hit that age and my attractions were toward my own gender. Plus, those attractions seemed fixed. I thought I was gay for life. But how could that be? I was a Christian.

Later I would come to a greater understanding of my dilemma—and undergo a change of heart, mind, and feelings. The point I want to make is that God didn't leap out of my heart because I was experiencing same-sex attractions. The thing about God is that He knew before He created me—certainly when He came into my heart at age six—that I would face a trial so great I would need Him more than ever. I believe needs send people to Christ. And those who perceive their same-sex attractions as a need that can draw them to God are on their way to wholeness.

The Bible says, "For God so loved the world that He gave His only begotten Son, that whoever [*anyone!*] believes in Him shall not perish, but have eternal life" (John 2:16 NASB).

That pretty much sums up nearly everything you need to know.

God takes the initiative by *loving* us. We respond to that love. And that's the invitation God offers each of us: to respond to His invitation to know and love Him.

So the most important question any of us—straight or gay—ever needs to ask is, "Have I come to the place in my life where I have confessed my sins, acknowledged my need for a Savior, and accepted God's forgiveness?"

If you're at that place now…if you don't know Christ and His freedom, you can do so right now. Before this chapter is finished, you can experience the love of God in a real way! You can begin the journey toward a better destiny than the one you're now on.

No matter what you've done in the past, God wants to have a relationship with you—just as you are now. We enter into this relationship by putting our faith in Christ. Will you pray right now, inviting Christ into your life…expressing your faith in Him and your desire to know Him and your choice to begin the journey toward wholeness?

God hears our hearts. Here is a suggested prayer, but feel free to add your own words, knowing God will hear every one…and He will answer with open arms.

Jesus, I come to You as a sinner, having made all sorts of mistakes. I realize I can't do this thing called life on my own. I need You to save me. I acknowledge that You are the one true Son of God and that You lived a perfect life and died a sinner's death so that I wouldn't have to. Thank You! Forgive me once and for all for my past, present, and future sins. I accept You as my Savior and embrace Your grace that will forever cover me. Thank You for this new life. Amen.

If you prayed that prayer with a sincere heart, please know that God heard it. At the moment you prayed and received Him, you became His child. You and I are now one in Christ! As your new brother in Christ, it will be my privilege to walk with you through the rest of this book and help you understand what a full and joyful life in Christ can look like as you surrender everything to the Lordship of Jesus Christ.

Congratulations, my friend. Accept God's love. Now allow the unfathomable nature of this gift to penetrate your deepest core and change you from the inside out. As you change on the inside, the outside will eventually follow.

You're no doubt wondering, *Okay, so I prayed the prayer. Am I going to going to start experiencing heterosexual desires? Will I continue to be tempted with same-sex feelings? And what do I do about my gay relationships?*

Good questions. And the rest of this book deals with expectations, change, and how you can make choices that will give you a better life. Giving your life to Christ is just the beginning. The changes happen as you *live* what you prayed.

As we move on to discuss what change looks like and how it happens, I encourage you to read with a pen, a notepad or journal, and a Bible at your side. Jot down notes, questions, and insights as we go along. God may bring things to your mind that will cause you to go "Aha!" about your past or present. At various points in the book, I'll also share my experiences that illustrate the concept under discussion.

I encourage you to pray before and while you're reading these chapters. This will help you really tap into what God has for you as you embark on your exciting new journey toward holiness and wholeness.

Got your pen, paper, and Bible? Okay!

Lord, I pray that this journey through Leaving Homosexuality *helps me see what You have for me. Help me understand the process of change that awaits me. Thank You for Your grace and mercy toward me. Thank You for making it easy to know and follow You. Amen.*

2

Developing Healthy and Realistic Expectations

What do you expect from God in relation to your same-sex attractions? Are you hoping for a 12-step program that will turn you into a heterosexual? Are you praying that you'll develop heterosexual desire to replace your homosexual desire?

I find that many people—including me many years ago—want a step-by-step guide to change from gay to straight. That isn't what this book is going to offer because no such plan exists. (Trust me. I searched for one for a long time.) I remember praying every night for over a decade for healing, change, freedom, and forgiveness. I was unsure how I had become gay, but I knew it was wrong and that I'd better do something to become *un*-gay. I have no idea what I thought God would do to accomplish that. But I do remember that I usually felt hopeless after a long night of intense, seemingly fruitless praying. Where were the changes I was praying for? Why was God so slow to act?

I think my hopelessness stemmed mostly from my belief about God—that He could not tolerate a gay child and would rather have anything but one of *those*. The constant unsettled feeling of not measuring up to what was expected of a boy—and a Christian one at that—was nearly too much for me to bear. Sadly, because of my deep fear of rejection and even retaliation, I ended up bearing that great burden all alone through almost my entire childhood.

How about you? You may not have had an early Christian experience as I did. But my guess is that anyone reading this book suffered through some sort of similar childhood struggle marked by the pain and loneliness of carrying this secret. No one should have to bear the weight of such a struggle alone, especially a child.

And maybe you're still bearing this burden alone. If so, you needn't do so any longer. The God who created you wants to take this heavy load from you. And, thankfully, He has provided help for you through churches, counselors, organizations such as Exodus International, and other excellent ministries.

I well remember the day I took that first step—and the false expectations I brought with me. I went to a local Exodus member ministry called "Exchange" in Winter Park, Florida. I sat down with the counselor and told him plainly that I expected God to make me straight. I conveyed to him in no uncertain terms that I wanted to be like other men. I told him I had been praying for years that God would fix this problem, and I was convinced that somehow He was going to do it through that ministry. I had no idea *how* it would happen, but I knew this was my only hope. I laid my list of unrealistic expectations on the table. I honestly wanted God to make me straight like my brothers and dad and all my friends. I wanted heterosexual feelings to replace the homosexual ones. I wanted to feel for women as I did for men.

> Strangely, this thorn of homosexuality has introduced me to my best friend, Jesus, who has made my life amazing and given it purpose.

That was long ago. And today change *has* come...but not quite in the way I expected. I have not "arrived" by any means, but I do have security in Christ today and a longing was fulfilled that changed my perspective on sexuality and, ultimately, on life.

The biggest change that has occurred is mostly related to how I view God and His grace. I no longer question God about my struggle. And I no longer wonder what purpose it has in my life.

It is what it is, I've concluded. I long ago dripped my last sweat bead from my brow worrying about why or how this struggle became mine. I just don't care how, what, or why. Instead, I see my early homosexual years as a time that—out of sheer desperation—drew me to God's love. Most people can't comprehend my attitude. But I often wonder, *If I hadn't had those desperate years, would I have sought Christ as eagerly? Had I not experienced those homosexual feelings, would I have fallen to my knees in prayer daily since I was 11 years old?* Sure, those juvenile prayers were a little misguided as I prayed that I wouldn't wake up gay the next day. But God, in His infinite wisdom, understood my immaturity and looked past the words of my prayer to the meaning behind it. He knew that if I kept praying for His perspective and His answer I'd eventually mature in my understanding of what I really needed to be praying about.

So, strangely, this thorn of homosexuality has introduced me to my best friend—Jesus—who has made my life amazing and given it purpose. Is this what's happening to you? Can you start to see your same-sex attraction as the very thing that causes you to cry out to God?

And if that which draws us to God should disappear entirely...would we still be as urgent in our dependency on Him? Realizing that God wants us to always remain dependent on Him will help us clarify the changes we can expect as we move away from our gay identities.

Realistic Expectations

Expectation is a double-edged sword. Expect too much or too little, and the outcome of either will trip you up.

There are two keys to using your expectations for good.

First, keep them realistic. Don't expect too much too fast. In my case, I set a six-month goal for healing. That was totally unrealistic. Also, heterosexuality shouldn't have been my goal—nor should it be yours. God's time frame in His work in us is very often different from ours. (By the way, if you're the parent of someone struggling or a spouse of someone battling same-sex attractions, this is especially critical to understand. Your loved one doesn't need the added pressure to conform to your timetable. Let God set the schedule, and then trust that He will help your loved one meet it.)

Second Corinthians 5:17 is a great verse that I often quote to new Christians: "If anyone is in Christ, he is a new creation; the old has gone, the new has come!" And though that's certainly true, I think we often incorrectly interpret this verse to mean that our Christianity is immune to our humanity. Basically we believe "Come to Jesus and life will be better instantly and completely."

Well, that's a nice and tidy way to look at it, but I don't know anyone who came to Jesus and found that their old ways and entire sin propensity were wiped out. Sure, we become new creations with a new eternal destiny, but that doesn't mean Jesus takes away our potential to sin. He didn't magically eradicate my same-sex attraction when I came to know Him. Remember, I came to Christ as a child and had no sexual attraction of any kind. That attraction developed three years later and precipitated more than a decade of deep and profound struggle. I came to Jesus, and when the same-sex attraction set in, my life got *worse.*

My point is simply this: There is no such thing as a struggle-free life. To have the expectation of life free from conflict is unrealistic. What *is* realistic is to expect to find new ways to deal with those struggles.

In the margin of my wife's well-worn and heavily written-in Bible is this key insight regarding 2 Corinthians 5:17: "*New*—refers to newness of *quality;* unrelated to *time.*" I love that because it sums up a very critical truth about God—who He is, how He created us, and our role in change. He didn't create us as His puppets. We have free choice to act. We can choose Him and invite Him into our hearts, and if we continue to daily choose His ways above our own, we have every potential for a new quality of life over time. Let me paraphrase 2 Corinthians 5:17 based on this understanding:

> Those who accept Christ are eternally secure and have the opportunity to not only exchange their eternities, but to

experience a changed life on earth over time as they choose His ways over their own. A new quality of life will come to fruition in God's timing as we make a life commitment to continually seek Him.

The second key to using your expectations for good is to allow your expectations to challenge and propel you. In other words, *don't expect too little*. Set goals that will make you work—and set goals that work.

For instance, a reasonable goal to work toward is *not* acquiring heterosexual lust. But a reasonable goal *is* to mature in Christ. As I often say, the opposite of homosexuality isn't heterosexuality; it's *holiness*. God wants you to pursue *His holiness* not heterosexuality. Become holy as He is holy (1 Peter 1:16), and you will become everything else He intends for you to be in the process.

Three Reasonable Expectations

There are three specific expectations to incorporate into your new life in Christ.

First is a life of obedience, which includes the biblical concept of self-denial. Self-denial has gotten a bad rap for a long time. When I was first starting out in ministry and sharing my testimony, I often heard the comment from gay individuals and activists, "You're just in denial, Alan." That comment always incensed me because it seemed to negate my message and my intelligence. However, as I began to really pray about it, I realized that we, as Christians, are indeed called to a life of denial, and as such I should not despise something the Lord commands of me nor should I get angry when someone calls me on it. Those who reject the concept of self-denial haven't reaped the joys that result from it.

Self-denial is found in several places in the Bible, including this verse in Matthew 16:24:

> *Then Jesus said to his disciples, "If anyone would come after me, he must* deny *himself* [disregard, lose sight of, forget own interests] *and take up his cross and follow me."*

Every day for more than a decade I have made denial, as Jesus taught in this verse, the major focus of my morning prayer time. I am keenly aware that I am prone to blowing it in this area of my life and am, therefore, in desperate need of help. For that reason, I have surrounded myself with people (especially my wife) who speak into my life boldly...and they do. But more important than these relationships is the one I have with the Lord, my Keeper. So every morning my prayer goes something like this:

Dear Lord, I cannot make it today without You. I need You to guide me, protect me, and help me make good decisions. I choose today to deny what comes naturally to me. I choose to pick up my cross and follow You. Amen.

And you know what? I love my life of denial. Ultimately it's my acknowledgement of my utter and profound weakness. And it is centered around a promise the Lord makes to us—that in our weakness His power is revealed. In 2 Corinthians 12:10, the apostle Paul wrote: "That is why, for Christ's sake, I delight in weaknesses, in insults, in hardships, in persecutions, in difficulties. For when I am weak, then I am strong."

> Our relationship with Christ doesn't remove the potential for temptation; it gives us the power to defeat it when it arises.

What freedom that brings me! I don't have to be perfect because *Jesus* is perfect. As I trust in Him and follow Him, I will be given strength to overcome whatever might be thrown at me.

I overcame the power same-sex attraction had over me when I chose to admit my weakness, to confess my need for a Savior, to accept Christ, and to deny my fleshly tendencies. *Wow!* God has been faithful to me too. By His grace I haven't fallen in more than a dozen years. That humbles me because I know that it has been and always will be *His strength* poured into my weakness that enables me to persevere.

Acknowledging our weaknesses is important because we are going to struggle with sin. We are human and will remain so until this life is over. Our relationship with Christ doesn't remove the potential for temptation, but it gives us the power to defeat it when it arises. Another powerful verse that can strengthen us during temptation is Philippians 4:13: "I can do everything through him who gives me strength." This verse doesn't say that nothing will come your way that you will need to overcome. It suggests you're going to experience some stuff and that you're going to need—and be given—the power to get through because of Christ. So expect trials.

John 16:33 is one of my favorite Bible verses, and I depended on it in the midst of some of my darkest trials as I fought to leave homosexuality.

> *I have told you these things, so that in me you may have peace. In this world you will have trouble. But take heart! I have overcome the world.*

Had I authored this verse I would have written it in all caps and put a video link beside it of me yelling it at the top of my lungs and waving my hands for emphasis!

When someone tries to tell you that Christians shouldn't experience trials and that if they do then something is amiss, turn to them and recite John 16:33. You *are* going to have trouble, but you most certainly can also have God's perfect and abiding peace (and strength) amid it. Smooth sailing in this life isn't assured. That's why Jesus teaches us to swim.

All Christians (in fact, all people) have issues to deal with. One of our issues has been homosexuality. So be it. It's part of being human to have something to contend with. Discipleship is part of how we contend with that which has been given to us. *A life of discipleship is a life that will not allow us to define ourselves by our sexual desires, but by our Creator.* As we submit those desires to Christ, we find freedom.

Expect Joy Incomparable

Lest you think the only things you can expect are obedience and self-denial, I am ending on my favorite note—a happy one. While I've come to love denial and discipleship, I have also come to love and know that as I'm obedient and deny the power of sin in my life I will experience great and abundant joy.

Homosexuality, like all sin, was pleasurable for a season (Hebrews 11:25). But I never experienced pure joy until I left the gay life behind. Happy indeed are those who finally realize that true happiness is not found in ordering life around same-sex attractions.

You will probably have some hard days—I know I still do. But I have peace and joy amid those difficult times like I never dreamed possible. I wouldn't go back to homosexuality for anything...no, not for *anything*! I wouldn't trade what I have now (the Lord, my wife, and my kids) for anything the gay life has to offer. Been there, done that.

Not too long ago Friday night rolled around and I had on my fat clothes (you know—elastic-waist shorts, big T-shirt, glasses only worn around the house with people who love you). We'd eaten pizza from a local Italian restaurant, the kids were bathed, Leslie was propped up on the couch, and it was almost DVD time. I said to her, "This is the life I treasure. It's my dream come true, and nothing could ever tempt me to leave it or you or them or my Jesus."

And I meant it. When I look at my family and compare that with where I could be right now, I marvel at God's goodness. Although I don't know what God has for you personally, I do know He has His best planned for you. That's one expectation you can depend on as you follow the Lord (Jeremiah 29:11).

Expect joy uncomparable, my friend. You can live on God's promises!

Expectations About Sexual Attraction

Are you wondering to what extent you can expect sexual attractions to change? Everyone's experience is different, but if you mean,

Will I become a stark raving heterosexual lust machine? The answer is no. Nor is that a good goal.

But if by "change" you're willing to first accept a changed heart and walk toward wholeness with God, you can expect any (or all) of these possibilities in the course of your future:

- *Diminished same-sex attraction.* To what degree it diminishes will vary. Some of you reading this book may continue to struggle with homosexual temptation for a long time. For others, less so. For some, you may find that God will eventually lead you to marriage. (More about that in chapter 6.)

- *Periods of fluctuating same-sex attractions.* New believers especially may undergo a "honeymoon" period where the joy of their newfound faith overpowers any same-sex attractions. Then, at some point, there is a return of the desires.

- *A lessening of importance on your sexuality overall.* Some Christians find that the sexual area of their lives, over time, becomes secondary to their spiritual lives. They find as they grow spiritually, the sexual issues are simply not the blazing forest fires of their pre-Christian experience. They also find that their spiritual growth enhances their relationships.

How God works with your sexual attractions is an individual matter. So don't look to the experience of others as a gauge for you. It's great to hear encouraging testimonies from other Christians who have achieved a level of success that has eluded you so far, but don't label yourself a failure. You're still growing!

Part 2

Moving into
Wholeness

3

The Power of Forgiveness

Luke 7:36-50 NASB

Now one of the Pharisees was requesting Him to dine with him, and He entered the Pharisee's house and reclined at the table.

And there was a woman in the city who was a sinner; and when she learned that He was reclining at the table in the Pharisee's house, she brought an alabaster vial of perfume, and standing behind Him at His feet, weeping, she began to wet His feet with her tears, and kept wiping them with the hair of her head, and kissing His feet and anointing them with the perfume.

Now when the Pharisee who had invited Him saw this, he said to himself, "If this man were a prophet He would know who and what sort of person this woman is who is touching Him, that she is a sinner."

And Jesus answered him, "Simon, I have something to say to you." And he replied, "Say it, Teacher."

"A moneylender had two debtors: one owed five hundred denarii, and the other fifty. When they were unable to repay, he graciously forgave them both. So which of them will love him more?"

Simon answered and said, "I suppose the one whom he forgave more."

And He said to him, "You have judged correctly."

Turning toward the woman, He said to Simon, "Do you see this woman? I entered your house; you gave Me no water for My feet, but she has wet My feet with her tears and wiped them with her hair. You gave Me no kiss; but she, since the time I came in, has not ceased to kiss My feet. You did not anoint My head with oil, but she anointed My feet with perfume. For this reason I say to you, her sins, which are many, have been forgiven, for she loved much; but he who is forgiven little, loves little."

Then He said to her, "Your sins have been forgiven."

It's so easy to take forgiveness for granted. What a mistake! Forgiveness is essential for emotional and physical health—and yet multitudes of people continue to harbor the bitterness that comes from unforgiveness.

If you're anything like me, you can recall instantly the most heinous of offenses committed against you. Forgiveness was hard for me. I was once one of the most offended and bitter people I knew. I wore my wounds like a shield. People could merely bump against me and I was reinjured. Not only was I bitter, I was angry too. Especially with my dad.

Dad was career military for 25 years before I was born. My mom and my four older siblings moved from state to state while Dad did his tours of duty. He retired from the Air Force two years before I was born and went into the restaurant and hotel business. My parents were in their forties when they found out they were going to have their sixth child. My oldest sister was already married with kids when I was born, one brother was in college, two siblings were in high school, and my next oldest brother was in kindergarten. I was a surprise obviously.

My mom was the classic mom. She was a Southern version of June Cleaver. She lived to serve her husband and kids. She should have won a mother-of-the-year award every year. All of us kids were, and remain, close to Mom. She is always easy to honor and love.

Dad, on the other hand, was a bear. He was a product of his military career and, before that, the Great Depression. He lost his own father while still a child and was routinely beaten by an older alcoholic brother. Dad's life wasn't easy.

While I only received about three memorable spankings from Dad, it was his day-to-day anger and roller-coaster moods that taught me early that I didn't want to be anything like him or be anywhere near him. He could be charming and fun and silly. He loved shopping and cars and houses, which I loved too. But I couldn't predict his huge mood swings.

I benefited from his highs. He loved to take us all shopping on Friday nights and always wanted me to have the very best of everything. But he could also turn those excursions into nightmares if something or someone set him off. I've been verbally ripped to shreds in department stores by my dad. And I've

> The taunting and name calling and constant bullying was endless.

seen him tear into salespeople and other patrons as the mood struck him. By the time I was six I hated Dad and vowed I would never be anything like him. He was the meanest man I knew.

Dad's temper ruined birthday parties, school functions, Christmas dinners, and other important gatherings. I can't speak for others in my family, but I venture to say that he wasn't anyone's favorite. We never knew which dad we were going to get or when the bad one was going to surface. It was awful.

I remember one family trip we took to visit aunts, uncles, and cousins in Tennessee. While there, a cousin I'd never met before said, "You look just like your dad." To which I curtly replied, "No, I don't. I look just like my mom."

In fact, to make sure I wasn't ever mistaken for a daddy's boy, I purposely mimicked every move my mother made. I sat the way she sat, ate the way she ate, and talked the way she talked. If my dad took a bite of something at dinner, I didn't take a bite at the same time. I waited to do it at the exact time my mother did. I watched how she used her napkin and did the same. I was determined to be my mother's son and get rid of any resemblance to Dad. This was my conscious mission for years.

Not surprisingly, my dad called me a sissy on more occasions than I care to remember. The anger I saw in his face during many encounters was blood curdling. In high school, when I was old enough to drive, I often left the house bawling over some argument we'd gotten into. I usually found solace at my sister's house. In those days I prayed my dad would die so I'd be rid of his mood swings and verbal assaults.

My dad was the worst…but he wasn't my only abuser. My peers teased me mercilessly, starting in fourth grade. Sixth grade was by far the worst year of my life. The taunting, name calling, and constant bullying were endless. Now, when I recall those terrible days, I pray for poor little dorky misfits like I was who are now enduring what I once did.

And to top off a pretty unhappy childhood, like so many others, around age ten I was molested by an older teenage boy. During those awful years escape and fantasy became my best friends.

Given all that, maybe you can understand why I might have a problem with forgiving—especially when there always seemed to be a new offense to get angry about before I had a chance to forgive the last one. The bathroom counter in my childhood home is loose to this day because after getting yelled at by my dad, I would retreat there. Amid silent tears, I'd try to rip off that countertop with all the strength I could muster.

A Turnaround

How did I learn and accept the importance of forgiveness in the healing process? It happened one Saturday morning in late June. I was at my first Exodus International Freedom Conference on the campus of Asbury Theological Seminary in Wilmore, Kentucky. During the last morning session God seemed to speak clearly as I sat daydreaming in the Estes Chapel balcony. He said, "Alan, I don't love you more or less than I love your dad. I love you both the same. The things that have hurt you aren't more grievous to me than the things that have hurt him. He is your brother in Christ more than he is your dad. I want you to forgive him."

For some reason, the thought of my dad being hurt as a child reduced me to a heap of tears. I'd never considered forgiving him, nor had I thought of him as a "brother" in Christ, even though I knew he professed faith in Jesus. I certainly never had considered that God would think my wounds were equal to anything my dad had suffered...until that momentous day. As strong as my hatred and bitterness had been only moments before was how fast and furious it was now pouring out of me in tears. I felt a strange and unexpected empathy and compassion toward a man I'd despised for a lifetime.

I knew I had to go home and tell my parents my story and release my dad from the offenses I'd held on to like a wad of thousand dollar bills. By this time in my life Dad had softened, and having made a profession of faith in Christ, he'd been going to church as often as the doors were open. He was still rough around the edges, but he was a lot easier to be around than he had been during my childhood years.

The day after that divine appointment in the balcony I was home in our family room telling Mom and Dad about my struggle. I said specifically to my dad, "How you raised me and related to me growing up had a negative impact on me, but I know you had a hard life too. I don't hold any of this against you. I'm sorry for how hard your life was, and I hope you can forgive me for how angry I've been."

My dad forgave me. He also said some really encouraging and life-changing things to me that day. My acknowledgement of his difficult life unlocked a basement door in his soul and out of it came stories of abuse—sexual, physical, and otherwise—that are too horrific for me to share here, let alone endure. The stories he told that day seemed endless, and by the end of them, I was surprised he'd turned out to be as good a man as he was.

He had worked hard and provided for his family, thinking that was the very best a man could offer. That afternoon I knew my list of grievances didn't even come close to comparing to what he'd gone through. The forgiveness that God had supernaturally birthed in my heart developed deep, deep roots that day.

As the weeks went by I noticed my dad, who was retired at that point, stared out the living room window a lot. I asked my mom if he was okay, and she said that he was grieving the lost years he'd missed with each of his children. She said that he felt my homosexual struggles were his fault and the pain was something he had to endure... something he felt he couldn't simply allow to pass.

I know he spent a lot of time praying in the months after that Sunday afternoon confession time. He also started a new ritual that was completely foreign to him and the rest of our family. He never let a day pass without telling my mom and all of his kids how much he loved them.

I moved out of the house early the next year and he called me every day. It even became annoying! He just wanted to tell me he loved me and was praying for me. He went from millitary drill sergeant to teddy bear Jesus freak almost overnight.

For the next 14 years my dad qualified for father of the year. He was everything I ever wanted and needed in a dad. Especially in his later years, he would just sit and hold my hand and look at me during our visits. I could see in his eyes pride and love and joy that I was his son.

> Forgiveness caused a refreshing rain to fall on the desert of my heart and turn it into a lush garden of love, grace, and mercy.

When it came to my testimony of overcoming homosexuality and my work with Exodus, my dad was one of my three biggest fans. My confession and forgiveness set him—and me—free. I can say without reservation that there will never be another man that I love like I loved my dad, nor is there anyone I am prouder to be like than I am him. I tried so hard not to be like him, but today I am the very best of him...just as God created me to be.

Forgiving my dad released me from that inner vow I'd made that I would never be like him or any other man. Forgiveness caused a refreshing rain to fall on the desert of my heart and turn it into a lush garden of love, grace, and mercy. I believe I truly became a man when I forgave my dad. I'd never wanted to be one before that point. But because of forgiveness, God restored what the locust had eaten (Joel 2:25).

Dad couldn't wait for Leslie and me to have kids. When we found out we were infertile, he was heartbroken for us and helped us in every way possible. When our kids, Isaac and Molly, were born, it was one of the happiest times in Dad's life. Seeing me become a father filled something in Dad's heart that changed him even more. He was a good father but an amazing grandfather.

At Dad's funeral in May of 2007, I was so proud to stand up and speak along with my siblings and declare that I hoped I would be as good a man as Dad was. I have life today because of him—and because God asked me to forgive.

Is Forgiveness Needed?

Who do you need to forgive?

Is it one person or many?

A parent? An abuser? A former partner? The "in crowd" at your high school?

Whoever it is, I encourage you to do it. Do it now.

Forgiveness may not come as suddenly as it did in my situation. You might need to wake up every day for years and forgive someone again and again until your heart is healed. God understands pain. He understands rejection too. And He forgives us for both.

You know, maybe you need to forgive yourself too. Maybe you even need to forgive God.

Whoever it is, do it. You won't be free until you do. You can't love unabashedly without forgiving those who have hurt you. And as it says in Luke 6:37, "Forgive and you will be forgiven." We *all* need forgiveness, and our willingness to forgive others is key.

Forgiving the Church

Many gays and lesbians need to forgive the Christian church. We

Christians haven't always demonstrated the love of Christ that we should have. In fact, if I had one thing to say to my fellow believers who are the body of Christ regarding how we have historically treated homosexuals it would be, "We were wrong in our attitudes and thus mishandled the situation." In the name of Christ many people helped create the angry and bitter Pro-gay Movement because of their pride and arrogance and un-Christlike heart toward people in need. Let's wake up. Let's repent of our hostility and recommit to boldly loving sinners as Christ did…and does.

The horror stories I've heard about the treatment some men and women have received at the hands of the Christian church are unbelievable. It's our job as the body of Christ to own our corporate mistakes and repent. We can't reach people in need if they distrust us based on their bad experiences with believers in Christ.

My friend Bill Merrell, former vice president of the Southern Baptist Convention Executive Committee, said at a press conference in Phoenix a couple of years ago, "We don't want a few churches with ministries to homosexuals. We want *every* church preaching, living, and loving like it should. *Only then are we doing our job.* Only then will we be assured of reaching everyone."

Ministries like Exodus International didn't exist in Corinth when homosexuals were changing as a result of the positive ministry of the church there. Here are some classic verses from the apostle Paul's first letter to the Corinthian church. He specifically notes the first-century same-sex people who had come to believe in Christ:

> Do you not know that the wicked will not inherit the kingdom of God? Do not be deceived: Neither the sexually immoral nor idolaters nor adulterers nor male prostitutes nor homosexual offenders nor thieves nor the greedy nor drunkards nor slanderers nor swindlers will inherit the kingdom of God. *And that is what some of you were. But you were washed, you were sanctified, you were justified in the name of the Lord Jesus Christ and by the Spirit of our God* (1 Corinthians 6:9-11).

That's the way it should be today—churches reaching out in compassion and presenting Christ as the one who washes, sanctifies (sets apart for Himself), and justifies people of all persuasions who give their lives to Him.

The sad result of the church's historic wrong attitude has been that many of you who are contemplating leaving or are leaving gay life may have allowed bitterness to take root because of the way the church mistreated you or those you know. Perhaps they've hurt, labeled, or rejected you, and you've seen a battle between "us" and "them." I believe many people affected by homosexuality have not moved as far forward as they would genuinely like to due to this faulty perception.

For your *own* sake, don't let bad church experiences—or bad experiences with Christians—keep you from all that's yours in Christ.

Forgive the Christian church.

Choose to forgive.

Choose to heal.

And if you get knocked down again by someone whom you've forgiven, get up and move on. And forgive again. God will help you!

If the church you visit in your new walk of faith doesn't "get" ministry to "us," find one that does.

The bottom line: A crucial aspect of moving on with your healing is to learn to be a really good forgiver. Forgiveness opens doors that have been locked and some you may not have even noticed.

4

A Life of Honesty and Acceptance

A key ingredient to a successful life is simple honesty. Like forgiveness, that too is a choice we make daily. I've seen what a failure to be honest can do, and that devastation has made me intentional about being honest in my life. I have way too much to lose to allow dishonesty to rob me of my family, my happiness, and my relationship with God. Being honest keeps me free from the things that once enslaved me. It also helps keep me headed in the right direction.

Honesty as it relates to the post-homosexual experience can be broken down into three categories—each one vital for our successful journey: honesty with ourselves, honesty with God, and honesty with others.

Telling Ourselves the Truth

Telling ourselves the truth about us is often one of life's greatest difficulties. It's easy to live in denial and fantasy, refusing to see our own brokenness and failure. When we aren't honest, we also tend to find ways to self-medicate our pain rather than deal with it. And, as many of us know from sad experience, self-medication can easily turn into addiction. (Whether it's alcohol, drugs, pornography, sexual encounters, or some other self-alteration, our human tendency is to go back for more and more...until it becomes an addiction. We become slaves to what we used for relief.)

Like many who are reading this book, the active gay life was one way I medicated or numbed my pain. Escape for me included pornography, masturbation, and sex with men (among other things).

Becoming a more dedicated Christian took away those forms of self-medication. I still have other potential self-medications when I'm tempted to believe I'm less than adequate as a husband, father, or leader, or somehow lacking in intellect, appearance, success, and so forth. Now my medication options are just more socially acceptable. Today they take the forms of more culturally palatable sin behaviors such as excess humor, excess shopping, home improvement projects, and even looking at catalogs—anything that allows me to live outside myself and my circumstances and helps me focus on something *I* can control.

> I developed a hard shell for protection from them... and from my self-hatred.

When we turn from reality to our favorite coping mechanisms, it's because facing the truth is painful. Who in their right mind wants to think about some of the things that people like you and me have experienced in our lives? Those experiences range from sexual abuse to verbal abuse, from physical abuse to violent, unspeakable traumas.

I can remember vowing to never again be publicly humiliated after years of being harshly and publicly corrected by my dad. And after years of being teased at school by peers who were fortunate enough not to have any outward flaws, I developed a hard shell for protection.

Those traumatic experiences led me to hate myself as a young person. And traumas like those lead us to retreat into our own safe worlds where we are in control and no one can hurt us.

A friend of mine recently confessed that he has lived his entire life trying to keep everything under control, from his finances to his personal appearance. He went on to say that early sexual abuse left him feeling out of control. The experience was so paralyzing that he spent his life ensuring he had order at all costs. This friend said he has no idea who he really is because he's been playing a part for so long he can't remember what life was like before he became obsessed with order.

I began the journey toward honesty during the first week I sought help for my struggle with homosexuality. At my first counseling appointment my counselor told me to start journaling daily. I took him seriously and went home and started writing in an inexpensive, red, spiral notebook.

I will never forget how incredibly difficult journaling was in those early days. I was so used to maintaining a facade that I actually had a hard time not lying in my journal. I wrote as if someone were going to eventually read it. I would over-explain and embellish. This was remarkably sad considering the only two who were ever going to see that journal (God and me) already knew the truth. Nonetheless, it took time for me to break the face-saving habit of lying, but eventually I did. I began to write everything that was on my heart and mind—good, bad, and hideously ugly.

I learned to be honest with myself. I learned that whenever I found myself wanting to escape from pain, I should right at that moment go to my journal and start "unpacking" what I was experiencing. What was sending me into a black hole so deep that I needed to escape? Through this choice to be honest, I learned to feel again. My escape mechanisms had been so ingrained that they automatically kicked in and numbed my feelings so I usually avoided what was distressing me.

I wasn't good at being honest at first. It took practice to say no to the easy and comfortable escape routes and instead choose to discipline myself to sit down at my notebook and process my feelings. Then I started by staying in the moment of my pain. I asked, "What am I feeling right now that is so horrible that I want to escape?" Choosing to feel the pain and being honest about how much it hurt, all the while doing so without my favorite escapes was excruciating. It was detox. I hated it. But a steady diet of that helped me make it a lifestyle that led to healthy relationships with God, me, and others. I soon learned to recognize patterns and head off the pain in healthy ways.

Today, 18 years later, I know what usually trips my triggers. As a result, some of those triggers no longer have much power. But, yes, there are still things that can blindside me. I know how to prepare

for them though. I know that if I'm hit with a pain so great that I feel
the need to escape, I can call for help or ask for prayer or go to lunch
with a friend or tell my wife that I'm wounded or do what I need to
do in order to heal and move on.

Going to God

I uncovered two profound insights in the process of journaling
and learning to be honest with myself. I could actually survive telling
myself the truth! And God didn't strike me dead for some of the things
I revealed to Him from the depths of my sad and lonely heart.

Journaling became my favorite way to pray. It was, in fact, my
stepping-stone to learning to pray. I found it very easy to yell at God
as I wrote, which taught me that He could handle my rage. I saw that
God is incredibly patient, has a high tolerance capacity, and offers
unlimited grace. If I had been God in those days I would have surely
hit the smite button on me more than once. But He didn't even consider it—never even came close!

Being honest with God taught me security. I learned to live for an
audience of One. I learned to care most about *His* opinion of me and
to believe what *He* said about me. I was also greatly blessed at that
time by reading *You Don't Have to Be Gay* by Jeff Konrad. Jeff encourages his readers to dig into the Bible to find out what God says about
them, so I did just that.

As I read the Bible and began to comprehend more about God's
heart for me, I came to realize there wasn't any reason not to be bru-
tally honest with Him. I learned that He wouldn't love me more or less
depending on my deeds, thoughts, and actions. I was finally beginning
to understand, as John says in his Gospel account, that I too am the
disciple Jesus loves! And if God loves me—a fallible human being—
with such an amazing and powerful love, then surely I can be honest
with Him. After all, He already knows my condition—knew it all
along and so loved me that He sent His Son so I could be free.

I guess the crux of what I learned about honesty with God is that
He loves me no matter what. He knows I can't do this thing called

life on my own, and so He invites me to rely on Him and to come to Him with the assurance that there is no condemnation awaiting me. His grace, mercy, and healing are ready. Why then should I ever fear going to Him?

Honesty with Others

For some reason, honesty with others has fallen on hard times today. Sometimes this is true even in the church, where honesty should be standard practice. Time and time again I hear horror stories of how church people have responded poorly to people seeking help. From public humiliation to gossip, from censure to being kicked out of fellowship, people have been condemned for simply admitting they were tempted to sin. But where else should we be able to go to be honest about our struggles than church?

Some people come to church week after week and when asked how they're doing, they reply using the Christian "F" word. You know the Christian "F" word, don't you?

"How are you this morning, Alan?"
"Oh, I'm *fine*, thanks." *Not!*

We aren't always fine, and we shouldn't hide that fact...especially in church.

My friend Joe Dallas talks about this in a story I love to hear and love to tell. When Joe was younger he worked in a restaurant that had a bar. On his regular shift as a waiter he was often working during that bar's happy hour. At first he would see the regulars come in every day and think, *How pathetic that they have nowhere else to go every afternoon but to this bar.*

Yet as time passed and he watched their easy camaraderie and openness, his opinion changed. He noticed that they would file in every day, turn the corner and scan the usual faces, and then exclaim, "Oh, thank God it's just you. People I can be honest with." These men and women, Joe came to realize, were some of the most honest people he had ever met. They came in daily and confessed marital issues, talked about their problems at work, and discussed family trials. They didn't struggle with authenticity. They were who they were with no apologies. And they accepted each other that way.

Before he knew it, Joe, a church-going Christian, began to envy the bar patrons and compared them to the people he knew at church who weren't as accepting of one another nor as honest. He thought, *What if I could walk into church on a Sunday morning, fling open the sanctuary doors, and say, "Thank God it's just you people. Those who know me and who accept me as I am." What if the church were more like a bar?*

God created us to be in community with each other. Community that is authentic, transparent, and honest. I found that at Exchange Ministries. Having grown up in a church where honesty was discouraged, it was nice to find a place where honesty was the whole point of being there. There isn't any reason to put yourself through the torture of going to counseling if you are just going to continue to hide.

> I got a taste of how incredible it is to live completely open with the facts that I am human, very fallible, and in need of a Savior.

Admitting my weaknesses was the biggest step anyway—nothing could be as difficult as that.

One day, having learned so many valuable lessons about honesty at Exchange, I put into practice being honest with others who weren't in my support group or leaders at my church who were helping me through this battle. New friends would ask me a question about something that would lead to me sharing what I was going through. I was cautious at first, worried about overwhelming people. At that point I was getting sufficient help and didn't feel the need to tell others my struggles to enlist their support. Some of the friends I told offered to help, and some of them I took up on their offers—whether to hold me accountable or just to have lunch on difficult days or simply hang out on nights that were old party nights at places I was trying to stay away from.

As I was developing that security in the Lord, caring more about what He said about me, and experiencing the freedom of telling others, I got a taste of how incredible it is to live completely open with the facts that I was human, very fallible, and in need of a Savior. I quickly got to the place where I didn't care who knew about my struggles. My sexual sin wasn't a scarlet letter to me anymore because it had transformed into a declaration of my need for Christ and the power of His grace and healing in my life.

Telling Family

I mentioned earlier about the day I became completely honest with my parents about my sexual struggles. Prior to that day they knew I'd been in counseling, and they even knew that the place I was going was primarily a place dealing with same-sex attractions. However, I had also told them it was the best place in town to deal with sexual abuse, which was the only part of my story I shared early on.

As I was maturing in my healing, I knew being totally honest with them was something the Lord was leading me to do and that it would be a healing moment for me. While I was aware that a negative reaction from Mom and Dad would hurt, I wasn't doing it for their reaction (good or bad). I was doing it as the next step in developing Alan Chambers' life of honesty and healing. I had prayed about this moment, and I knew others were praying for me.

As I've previously shared, telling Mom and Dad led to wonderful healing. I truly believe it was a major event in my growth into manhood. Sitting down with my mom *and* dad was a big step. I usually opted to tell Mom and let her pass things on to Dad. But sitting with Dad man-to-man was *huge* because of our poor relationship. I was nervous but not afraid. I was calm and I shared my story as matter of factly as possible, without any anger or accusation.

I knew my parents didn't want to hear such a confession, but I also knew they wouldn't be totally surprised by it. They affirmed their love for me—no matter what—and told me how proud they were that I had decided, on my own initiative, to get godly and biblical help from others.

So now one of my brothers and his wife and my parents knew. My support team was growing. Next I told another brother and his wife. Then another. I told my sisters last. Telling my story wasn't easy because of the content and because back then stories of freedom from homosexuality weren't common. But God gave me the words, and finally my entire family knew. The information sharing changed us. It bred honesty among people who had been content, like most other families, to sweep things under the rug.

Perfection Isn't Possible

Recently a friend of mine, after seemingly walking in freedom from homosexual behaviors for seven years, left his wife and kids and moved in with his gay lover. He told his wife that he had been in and out of the gay life for years. People were aware of his testimony about leaving homosexuality. His wife knew. His friends knew. His church knew. He had even had an affair early in his marriage but was restored. He had openly and honestly shared so many dark secrets that it seemed like a given that he would continue to be honest.

But he wasn't. I can only conjecture that he got through the crisis of that early affair and stopped being honest about the little things—a thought here, a look there. Knowing him, he probably didn't have an Internet filter or a form of accountability set up for avoiding far too easily accessible pornography. He took care of the family finances so who, other than him, was going to know what was on his credit card bill? A compromise here led to a compromise there, and before he knew it years of compromise and dishonesty led to what looks like the end of his marriage and the devastation of his kids. I could sit here and judge him, but I understand how easy it is to stop talking, stop being honest and transparent, and stop letting others help with accountability.

I see his situation as one more reminder of the importance of honesty in my life. I don't want my life to resemble his. I know that no one, including me, will get to the place where he or she is beyond the reach of temptation. Circumstances happen. Events occur that set us up for failure. We have to know ahead of time how to respond when someone—even someone we love, such as a family member—ticks us off (as we do them). Or when something at work upsets us. Or somebody cuts us off in traffic. Or all of these occur on one day. Or someone we know is dying. Something is going to happen. We're not always going to be fine. Life isn't going to be smooth sailing all the time. And when it isn't, let's be honest about it.

What's the harm in saying, "I'm tempted to look at pornography today. Please help me. Please hold me accountable. Please call me tonight." Or "I'm tempted to do that…." "I just did this…." "I miss the excitement of this temptation."

When we're not honest, the enemy can find a foothold in our lives, and he will use it to gain an even stronger position. And if we allow the process to continue, sin will become a tree with roots that are very difficult to pull up.

Be honest, my friend. Choose to care most about what your Lord says about you. Allow that to breed security and wholeness in your life. This will help you stand strong against the accuser and any voices of doubt. Allow the Lord to teach you to stand up in Him and proclaim who you really are—His! Be honest about what you are capable of.

The Power of Acceptance

Another major step forward in the journey out of homosexuality is when we accept ourselves as God made us. And even more, accept ourselves with joy and expectation for *all* that God means for us to be. This was certainly a tough issue for me.

I was born a boy, but from my earliest memory I wanted to be something else. The first shoes I could walk in were a pair of white pumps. As early as three or four I was raiding my sister's closet and pretending to be her little sister. I was mistakenly forming the identity of a girl. For reasons I wasn't aware of and that were not my fault, I was accepting an identity that was not what God had designed for me.

I learned to escape into a world of make-believe. In that make-believe world, I was a girl. I learned to process everything around me as a girl. I pretended to be a girl everywhere I went, even in crowded rooms where people were unaware of my inner world. Sometimes I was mistaken for a girl, which validated my beliefs but also crushed and embarrassed me. While I wanted to be a girl, I knew I wasn't… and that I couldn't ever be one. It was a tortured life.

My interests as a kid were all centered around make-believe too. I loved playing house with my friends. I loved playing with Legos and building elaborate homes and neighborhoods (I had a *lot* of Legos) for the girl character I pretended I was. I liked to shop and decorate my room and even the whole house. And I was good at it. I would tell my mom that I would dust the furniture just so I could put things where I liked them to be.

All of those interests, while very enjoyable for me, were ever-present reminders that I was different. My brothers didn't like any of those things, and neither did my male friends at school. My dad liked to shop but he loved "real man" things more—football and baseball, for example. I hated those things.

As is often true, kids can be cruel. And if your experience was anything like mine, your friends never let you forget how different you were. Although I never divulged my love of decorating or other "feminine" interests to my peers, they easily picked up on the fact that I was different. By the time I entered sixth grade, that difference earned me the label "gay." Sadly, but finally, my difference had a label.

The desire to be accepted by others was strong, and I began a crusade to become socially acceptable. I pretended to like things I didn't like. I developed an incredible sense of humor that my peers—even my enemies—loved. I hid every part of me that could be construed as gay. I did a pretty good job because I eventually became moderately popular.

This quest for social acceptance affected every area of my life. It became my constant desire, and everything I said or did was filtered through it. I said things I knew people would like or laugh at. I dressed in a way that got positive attention and even envy. I didn't just want to be accepted by others; I wanted to be acceptable to myself. I liked who I was becoming outwardly. Inwardly I was a mess—a controlled mess though.

Our culture punishes anyone who doesn't fit the "standard" mold. If you are born a boy, you are expected to love and excel at sports. You should also be handsome. But if you aren't, you'd better be strong and able to bond with your male peers over manly things like cars or objectifying girls or something "normal" like that. I tried doing that, and I bet many of you men reading this did too. And you women, What did you do as a young person to fit in? Was it torture for you too? As I think back, I roll my eyes over those days and am so thankful they're long gone.

And the gay culture has its expectations too. The need to look attractive and be desirable is considered a huge asset in the quest for acceptance, particularly the kind of acceptance that leads to intimate encounters. Without that desirability, a gay man or woman will face a high level of rejection when seeking acceptance.

It seems ironic to me now, but when I first set foot in a ministry for men trying to overcome homosexuality, the men I met with became very protective of me...even fatherly. They didn't want to see me go through what they did or do the things they had done before leaving homosexuality. If they'd known how much I craved doing what they had experienced, I think they might have put me under lock and key.

The guys were always telling me they wished they could go back and be as innocent as I was. Funny, all I wanted was what they had. *Homosexuality might be wrong,* I often thought, *but how will I know it won't meet that aching need inside my heart if I never try it?* Every story I heard in that support group and every event confessed by my accountability partner pushed me one step closer to searching out my own experiences. As I type this, I wish I could be transported back in time to tell the young Alan Chambers what I know today. I wish I could spare him the heartache and pain of looking for acceptance, wholeness, and meaning in meaningless places. I wish I could go back and tell him not to look for hope in hopeless environments. Unfortunately I eventually decided to participate in gay life.

The first night I ventured out to a gay bar, I remember getting pretty drunk and being overwhelmed by the sheer number of gay men in the place. I felt strangely at home...and yet not. It was almost like I'd been handicapped my whole life and made fun of for that fact, yet when I opened the door to this place and saw all the people inside... they too were handicapped. And when they saw me in my "wheelchair," they explained that I'd been born handicapped and that it was okay and that I should accept and even celebrate it. The gay friends I made never once wanted to alter anything about me, which was a nice change after growing up in a church environment where everyone seemed to expect perfection or at least didn't share real-life struggles of a personal nature.

Despite my best efforts, no one hit on me that first night out. I did stalk a few really good-looking guys. I remember driving home alone and feeling disappointed, empty, and extremely sad. I also felt a loss of innocence. All I'd done was go to a gay bar, gawk at guys, and get a little drunk. The "up" side was that I'd become a member of a club that accepted me. This was new and exciting! I was determined to go back and try to get more fun out of it. But I also wondered if it really got any better than what I'd experienced. I liked my new friends, for sure, but they weren't in the running for the happiest people in the world. They were nice looking and successful, and a couple of them were in relationships. But they weren't quite how I would have defined "happy."

When I got home that night and crawled into the bed of my youth, in the room of my childhood, I was different. I'd deceived my parents and was definitely not a momma's little boy anymore. I wasn't the guy my high school or church friends knew either. I was someone I didn't know very well. And I knew life wouldn't ever be the same. Regardless of how good or bad homosexuality turned out to be, I was going to live it.

I spent the entire next day preparing and thinking about going out again. I nailed down my plans, convinced my new friends to meet me at the same bar, and dreamed of the exciting possibilities. This would soon become a ritual for me. I called it "the hunt." I was like an animal on the prowl for food, for sustenance. Going to the bars was my feeding ground, and men were my prey. I loved preparing for the hunt…it was invigorating and exciting. The fantasy of what I would find was intoxicating. I couldn't wait to live it. I didn't know it in the beginning, but I later realized that the hunt was the best part. Why? Because I either wouldn't find what I wanted and would go home alone or I'd find something that seemed perfect. (Except when I embraced it, I realized how far from perfect it truly was.)

Months of this cyclical ritual left me emptier than when I'd started, but I was absolutely hooked on the adrenaline rush. My friend Mary Heathman would later tell me that the definition of addiction is needing more and more to get less and less. That was me. I needed more of the high to even experience a little of it. More hunting. More sex. More fantasy. More masturbation. New ways of achieving all of it. I was definitely addicted. And I had lost something precious—and I knew it. My desire to be accepted—and to accept myself wasn't happening either.

I think my road to acceptance began with a man named Kirk and the other Christian men who befriended me during the early days of my journey out of homosexuality. You'll read more about them later. But it was in those days and with those men that I began allowing others to see who I really was. They already knew the "big" issue—same-sex attraction—so I thought why not allow them to see more of me? It's weird, but even though homosexuality is often the big cultural stigma that sends so many to the closet, it's the deeper things—the more personal ones so intimately and intricately connected with *who* we are—that are hardest to share.

Through these men I began accepting I was a male. Their fellowship and *acceptance* of me as a fellow man were powerful agents of change and self-acceptance. It was a real break from the counterfeit reality I had been living.

We seemingly go into the closet to hide our homosexuality. But maybe what we're really hiding from others is even more than that.

Maybe we're hiding (and not accepting) who we are—who God created us to be, our very beings. Interestingly, in the biblical account of creation, Adam and Eve "went into the closet," so to speak, to hide from God.

And when people can't stay in the closet any longer and they "come out," it's often less about the sex than it is about their sense of being. Again, people say they are coming out of the closet as "gay," but they are really coming out in a much deeper sense. Their God-given gifts and talents and personalities come out too. Those things that they hated in themselves, thanks in part to gender and cultural stereotyping, emerge. For instance, my decorating skills were no longer a secret.

> I finally stopped hating—and instead began accepting—who God created me to be. I began loving how uniquely I was made and boldly being a man who loved beauty.

The real coming out for me involved getting out of homosexuality and accepting who God truly created me to be. I came out of my denial that I was created to be a man. And that went beyond the fact I have a penis. I was innately, characteristically, spiritually, genetically, physically, emotionally, and psychologically a man. I came out of the deception that to be a man means to be a womanizer, sports fanatic, and tough guy. I came out of self-hatred of being a touchy-feely man who could easily cry and be hurt. I came out of the fear of showing my real self to people. Their opinions didn't matter in light of what God thought about me and what *I* thought about me.

I was healed of the inadequacies and insecurities that led me to believe that someone like me couldn't be the kind of man to a woman that I would need to be. I came out of the need to have another man be that for me. I accepted the fact that I am not and never will be perfect. I came to understand that my perfect ideal of a man (that I once craved sex with) was just as inadequate and imperfect as I was.

I finally stopped hating—and instead began accepting—who God created me to be. I began loving how uniquely I was made and boldly being a man who loved beauty and could pick it out quickly. I stopped perverting that gift by objectifying beautiful men and began blessing the ways that God made them beautiful. I stopped worshiping what I thought was ideal and began enjoying the traits in me that I had been cursing as "less than."

I came out all right, but more than that I came *into* a place that I will never leave and that will only get better. I'm not perfect and I have struggles, but I love who I am because I am who God made me. I could not truly love others until I loved myself as God loves me. This is true acceptance—not of what I do, but of who I am in Christ.

I want you to come to this place of utter acceptance of how God sees you. And that will include full acceptance of your gender assignment. Forget the images of perfection and traits that society assigns your given gender. They are only illusions. Simply come to the place of acceptance of who you are in God. Let God mold the clay vessel that you are into the man or woman He envisions.

Self-acceptance is another important marker on the road to freedom from homosexuality.

5

Finding Authentic Community

As critics are all too quick to point out, some men and women who make professions of faith and leave the gay-identified world eventually return to homosexuality. One critical reason this happens is because the person who left the gay life doesn't find an adequate level of support in his or her new life. Often the church community isn't as accepting as the gay community.

And people were created for community. It's hard-wired into our beings by the God who made us. We *must* have it to become and remain healthy. Community is a major food necessity for our hungry souls. We can live without sex, but we can't live without real, authentic, transparent, *relational* community.

To understand this foundational need we have for community, let's take a good look at who God is and how He chose to create us.

The very existence of God screams "relational." He is the "Three in One," the Trinity, the Father, the Son, and the Holy Spirit. Knowing that God, in His very core, is relational helps us to understand the creation process.

For instance, God stated very quickly after making Adam, "It *is not good* for the *man* to be *alone;* I will make him a helper suitable for him" (Genesis 2:18 NASB). That declaration has many deep revelations. First, it speaks to the fact that God knows fellowship is vital. *We need each other*. Relationship, camaraderie, and intimacy are gifts that breed healthy life. Man left alone, without relationship, isn't good and sets us up for deep struggle. A water glass was meant to hold water. We humans were meant to be filled with the Lord and with healthy relationships.

God did not create you capable of meeting your own relational needs. It's His intent that *He* is the primary source of fulfilling our relational needs. We build on that foundation as we relate to others, who are meant to supplement our need for relationship. Men and women leaving homosexuality need healthy, transparent, authentic, same-sex relationships.

I think that all anyone needs to do to see how relationally starved our society has become is to look at the way sex has been offered as a substitute for real relationship. Sexuality is present in everything from Uncle Ben's Wild Rice commercials to the music we hear on the radio. In our culture, sex has become the counterfeit to true intimacy.

Upwards of 65 percent of Christian men struggle with Internet pornography because it's instant "relationship" without any of the work. Pornography for women is available in trashy novels or soap operas that allow an escape into fantasy and false intimacy.

> Community is essential to long-term success and wholeness. You can't do life successfully by yourself.

We crave what God created us to have...and yet we so readily accept a counterfeit. When someone falls back into homosexuality, I can't help but think they're still expecting to find satisfying intimacy in the wrong places. I also wonder how they failed to find true intimacy in their Christian walk. Was it too much trouble? Could they not find a supportive church? Did Christians fail them in some way?

There's no doubt that acting out sexually is an easy—but extremely fleeting—fix for pain caused by no intimacy. But the speed that such acting out becomes first a habit and then a lifestyle makes it dangerous. Have you realized that a life of brief sexual encounters or even extended same-sex relationships doesn't ultimately make for a life of relational satisfaction? I know for me—and possibly for you—I acted out sexually because it was easily accessible and I was starving. Remember...

- *God is a relational God.* To be in relationship with Him and to be in relationship with others is at the core of who He is and who He created you to be.

- *Community is essential to long-term success and wholeness.* You can't do life successfully by yourself.

The Stepping-stone

In the very early days of my recovery I was looking for community anywhere I could find it. As I mentioned earlier, Exchange, a local Exodus ministry, became my community initially. There I learned I was safe to share the depths of my heart and struggle without fear of backlash. The people in my support groups understood the need for confidentiality. Anything any of us shared stayed in that room. It was such a relief to have somewhere to go to unload a decade's worth of secrets to people who understood because they had been there too.

Exchange became my community for a time. These people were the ones I trusted most, and who, ultimately, even in a few short weeks, knew more about me than anyone else in the world. I didn't realize it then, but that ministry and the people in it were helping to heal each other (including me) through the power of authentic community. While I had grown up a very social and well-connected person, I wasn't really known and, therefore, wasn't truly accepted.

Let me camp out on that for a moment.

When you're harboring a secret, you begin to define yourself by that secret—to judge yourself and your relationships based on that secret. So if someone knows your secret and professes love or friendship for you anyway, then you know he or she truly must love you. That kind of love penetrates into your deepest core, meeting your love needs.

If someone who doesn't know your secret says you are loved, you often wonder, *What if he knew my secret? Would he still feel the same way?* I call this the "If they only knew" syndrome. In my life, at the time I found Exchange, no one else knew my struggles. Therefore, all the love professed or shown by friends and family failed to reach my deepest needs. I felt loved but not accepted because they didn't know the "real" me.

Exchange was a great place to begin building community. The leaders there knew that such community should only be temporary, however. They knew the ex-gay community could easily become a place of plateau and eventually even stall growth. To stay in the safe haven of my ex-gay compadres could easily become an unhealthy parallel to a nonsexual gay community. So Exchange did for me what I now do for others: They pointed me to the true community—to the Christian church. They wisely let me know I couldn't stay in their support groups forever. I couldn't go to counseling forever. They encouraged me to go to church. The church is where you should be able to walk out your long-term success surrounded by a community of believers that accept you and encourage you to grow.

Finding My Church

I believe some people go back to homosexuality because they don't find something better in the church. My friend Sy Rogers hit the nail on the head when he said, "I didn't leave homosexuality because it was so bad. I left homosexuality because I found something better." He wasn't referring to sex, but more to the gay community, which was what he knew. And the "better" Sy found wasn't heterosexuality, per se, but authentic community that can only be found in Jesus and the body of Christ.

My life will never be the same because of the community I found in the people at Discovery Church in Orlando, Florida. I was struggling with whether or not I was going to keep fighting homosexual desires or chuck the agony and completely embrace the gay life. By then I had become friends with openly gay men. Men with feelings like mine. As with so many others who understand that initial exhilaration of meeting like-minded people, I saw an opportunity for relationship there.

Finally being able to be honest about my struggles with the people at Exchange Ministries and my new openly gay friends left me disinterested in being at my church, a place I knew I wouldn't ever share my personal battles. So more often than not, I skipped church or visited the church where some of my Exchange friends attended. I was now 20 years old, living a life of secrecy, fearing my Christian world would find out about my foray into gay life. I wasn't yet ready to tell the whole world, but I was eager to find a new community of people with whom I could be open about my very real and present homosexual issues. I wanted to decide which lifestyle to embrace—the gay-identified one or the one being modeled by the leaders at Exchange.

One afternoon I met with my three older brothers, none of whom I was particularly close to. I didn't have much in common with any of them. Nonetheless, we got together for lunch that day. When we'd finished our meal, my next oldest brother asked me to run his leftovers by his house on my way home.

When I arrived at his house, I knocked on the door and my sister-in-law took the leftovers. She asked if I wanted to come in. I did. Very quickly into our conversation she asked me directly, "I've often wondered whether you are more attracted to men or women."

My first thought was, *Well, don't beat around the bush. Just come out with it.* A bit shocked, I stammered and stuttered for a minute.

She followed up with, "It's okay. I'm not going to judge you. I just want you to know I care and would love for you to come to church with us."

I was familiar with their church, and I had attended a service or two a few years prior. My sister-in-law told me that it was a very understanding and welcoming church. She mentioned that there were dozens of people who had struggled with homosexuality and overcome it. She said I would love it and told me if I wanted to come I could ride with her and the kids to the Wednesday evening service that night.

I agreed to go because I really wanted to and because there were some people there who had been friends with one of my much older brothers. The pastor of the church also knew my other brother. The thought that there were Christians from my past who might also be okay with my current struggle was strangely comforting and intriguing.

Going to Discovery Church that night was, in an odd and different way, as exciting as the night I went to my first gay bar. I was nervous. I think it was because I hoped my time at Discovery would be life-changing. It was. That night I knew the Lord was telling me to come back on Sunday…and every Sunday after that for a long time. It felt like home in a new, hip sort of way. I ended up going back the following Sunday morning and again on Sunday night and then again the following Wednesday. I loved the worship, I loved the messages, and I especially loved the people who opened their arms to me.

I became especially connected to a man named Kirk. Kirk was, and still is, a guy's guy. Married. A father of three. Leader. Athlete. And Kirk liked me. He was one of the first people who talked to me at the church and, like my sister-in-law, seemed to be able to see the blinking gay light on my forehead. He invited me to come talk to him and another leader, whom I knew.

Not too many weeks into my time at Discovery I had what they called a "Ministry Time" with Kirk and the other leader. Kirk led it. He basically just asked me to share my hurts. What a thing to ask!

I poured out my heart. I shared hurts related to being angry with my dad. I talked about being ridiculed and made fun of by my peers. I confessed hurt over not being like my brothers or even feeling accepted by them. All of this got to the core of my gaping and deeply infected wound of needing a man to love me, which sure was something that fueled my struggle with homosexuality. I remember craving the simple nonsexual touch and embrace of a man and spending hours fantasizing about such encounters. I had wanted that since I was very young. And I know some of you reading this can relate.

Confessing that need reduced me to a bawling heap. And that's when something I never would have imagined happened. Kirk reached out and embraced me. It wasn't premeditated or contrived. It was like a father reaching out for his son. It was my heavenly Father reaching out for me. Kirk hugged me and I sobbed. In Matthew 5:4, one of the beatitudes says, "Blessed are those who mourn, for they will be comforted." Never had mourning felt so good to me.

I'd never felt such comfort from a man...from a father...as I did that afternoon. I spent many hours crying with Kirk and the other leader that day. Kirk spent the time simply letting me weep on his shoulder. It was one of the most satisfying times of my life. Even now, as I remember that day, I feel a centeredness and peace and comfort. It was so remarkable! I knew it was God the Father hugging me through this man.

I left that ministry time changed. A longing I had experienced for more than a decade was fulfilled in a healthy, godly way by a healthy, godly man who didn't have any ulterior motives. Nor did he shriek or jerk back in horror at the gay guy who was reaching to embrace him as if letting go would mean falling thousands of feet to his death.

Emotionally, it was a life-or-death situation for me. Literally I felt re-fathered. I know that might sound kooky, but today I am a father, and I love hugging my son and daughter. I love to snuggle with them at bedtime, during their morning chocolate-milk ritual, or anytime those active kids let their dad hold them. I know how centering and special it is for them to know their dad loves them. Well, that day at Discovery, 20-year-old Alan Chambers had an experience like that for the first time.

Thus began my season at Discovery Church, a place where "community" became my reality. I quickly came out to everyone there. It wasn't a secret anyway, and no one seemed to really care. My story was common there. There was every kind of "former" you could imagine. My sin wasn't a big deal because the people at the church categorized all sin the same way. It was a little hard to adjust to. I was used to fearing what people thought, but here my homosexuality was just another item on the list of what Jesus could heal.

Discovery Church was a hospital for me—but a hospital that quickly became a medical school. They facilitated a process that helped me heal in ways I never dreamed possible. In time that hospital became a university that trained me to be a doctor, to do what they had done for me with others. They trained me to share and point people to the truth. Church is where healing and wholeness occurs.

I wish I could say it will be easy for you to find your own Discovery Church, but it may not be. You'll need to pray, ask around, and visit ministries and churches until you have that sense that "this is home."

I spent three-and-a-half years at Discovery before the Lord moved me to a new church that I helped transform into a similar hospital-turned-med-school environment.

When the Going Gets Tough

My friend Andy Comiskey often says, "I've been to hell and back in the church, but I'm still in the church." Church is a bunch of human people. They're going to make you mad, and they're going to frustrate you, and they're going to upset you. And sometimes they're going to be ignorant and say stupid things. But you know what? We *all* say stupid things. We all say ignorant things. We all do dumb things. *Forgive.* Get past it. Get over it. Stay in the church.

> I believe that if you are committed to living out the truth, God will lead you to authentic people and to authentic community where you can heal... and then help others heal.

To be honest, there aren't a lot of churches that "get" homosexuality. There are some that may not totally understand homosexuality, but they do understand grace and will easily incorporate a person struggling with homosexuality into the grace perspective. Thankfully, that's becoming more common. Unfortunately, far more often the church and Christians don't understand. They may have a heart for people caught in sin, but they don't know how to talk to someone affected by homosexuality or what *not* to say when talking about homosexuality. Please give them as much grace as you would like to receive from them.

The truth is that you, even in your broken state, might be God's answer for a church—the answer to the congregation becoming a more compassionate and caring community. But you will probably need to be patient...and so will they.

Above all, pray for God to guide you to authentic community.

Kirk once told me that if I needed him, he would do anything for me...but I had to *ask*. He also told me that it didn't matter where I was, what I had done, or even if I was out doing it the moment before church started on a Sunday or a Wednesday. I just needed to make sure I got to church when the doors were open.

I often took him up on that offer. In those early days of my walk, there were Sunday mornings that I came to church having stayed out looking for sex the entire night before. Even then, I would always get up that next morning, get dressed, and come to church—often just sitting through the entire service so I could drag myself over to Kirk afterward and cry on his shoulder. He let me, but he also talked to me like a dad would his son, telling me that what I was doing could not last forever and that I needed to do what I knew was right. He (and through him, God) was speaking truth into my life.

I believe that if you are committed to living out the truth, God will lead you to authentic people and to authentic community where you can heal...and then help others heal.

6

Dating, Marriage, and Yes...Sex

As early as age 11 I realized that the gender insecurity I'd felt since about age 4 had resulted in me being exclusively attracted to members of my sex. I hadn't asked for same-sex attractions, I didn't want them, and no matter how hard I prayed they didn't go away. I was praying not just because I didn't want those attractions, but also because even at that age I knew I wanted more from life than what those attractions offered.

I wanted a family. I wanted to have kids. Given my attractions, my misdirected options included being a "house husband" to a strong, secure man. Yet deep down inside, I wanted to be that strong, secure man. My dream was to be emotionally capable of loving a wife and family. Naturally I was confused and discouraged because of my leanings. And so I endured an intense battle with my sexuality for the majority of my childhood and into early adulthood. I never stopped praying to become a well-adjusted, "normal" man with a wife and kids.

There were days that dream was in jeopardy, but I fought for it to survive with everything inside me. I didn't want to settle for just *any* relationship. I wanted the ideal relationship. I didn't expect perfection... a relationship without conflict or adjustments. I wanted the real deal. Settling instead for a close homosexual relationship was tempting, and had gay marriage been legal in those days, I might have faced a greater pull to give up my dream. Thankfully, that distracting detour wasn't an option, so I kept fighting. Some days the only fight I had in me was just enough to maintain a seed of hope.

Ultimately, everyone decides the kind of life they want. And many of us who found ourselves caught in attractions we didn't choose or want *decided* to pursue a better life than what homosexuality offered. Presumably that's why you're still reading this book. You want something better. And that something better may or may not include a family. Not everyone is called to heterosexual marriage and kids. Some who leave homosexuality do so simply because they're done with the false glitter of gay life.

What's Your Goal?

Pursuing heterosexuality might be your desire, and it is God's best for human sexual expression (within the confines of marriage). But a specific sexual orientation isn't the ultimate make-or-break issue in life. I'll say it again because this is critical: Heterosexuality isn't your goal.

God created the man–woman ideal relationship, but as post Adam and Eve human beings, we are imperfect and must submit our imperfections to God to either heal or teach us to survive with the limitations. That is what I and thousands of others have chosen to do with our sexuality. I may be emotionally, relationally, and sexually limited, but I am spiritually able, through Christ, to live beyond those circumstances. So are you.

> Pursuing holiness will change your heart, which will change your life and your circumstances.

While heterosexuality may be what we were originally created to enjoy, God certainly gives us the power to live a wonderful life beyond a struggle with homosexuality. It's only as we choose to be defined by our sexual attractions that we become limited. Consider that you are far more than your sexual impulses. The potential for happiness is found in that "far more" aspect of your being. It's *not* found in either homosexuality *or* heterosexuality.

So, if the goal is not heterosexuality, what is it? Having entered into a relationship with Christ, *holiness* becomes the goal. "Holiness" is a very religious and scary word in some ways. But what it suggests is being set apart for God's purposes. And as you consider this as your goal, you will find that it's really the key to change in your life. As you pursue holiness, *God will change you from the inside out.*

Behaving heterosexually won't change your homosexual struggles. Acting "culturally straight" won't make you anything but a good actor. But pursuing holiness will change your heart, which will change your life and your circumstances. Notice that I didn't say pursuing holiness will bring about heterosexual attractions. Again, that's not the point. In His great wisdom, understanding, and timing, God will give you His best. Pursue holiness over heterosexuality. Pursue holiness over homosexuality. Trust God for the changes that will come.

What About Dating and Marriage?

Around the fourth year of my journey toward holiness and out of homosexuality, I was still struggling with some serious sexual and emotional issues. I was making progress, but I wasn't completely free. I was falling to temptation and getting up, but still falling nonetheless. I was, however, also beginning to experience a desire for a relationship with a woman. It wasn't sexually motivated in the least, but I did have a desire to emotionally connect with someone with whom I was truly compatible.

Let me stop here for a moment and make a critical comparison and confession. I was living with a fellow Christian brother who was also trying to find freedom from homosexuality. While he was someone I considered a friend and brother in Christ, I was emotionally and sexually attracted to him.

Our relationship was anything but healthy and was hindering me finding the freedom I was looking for. One part of me wanted a life-long relationship with this man. That desire, and everything that went along with it, was marked by turmoil, possessiveness, jealousy, envy, and unhealthy comparisons. What I perceived I would gain from a relationship with him was defined by everything I perceived I was lacking.

In hindsight, that man wasn't a complement to me as I thought he was. He was me—or what I wanted me to be. I wanted him to be the component I was missing. As sometimes happens in homosexual relationships, it was becoming emotionally addictive. It was at its core selfish, self-serving, and self-focused. And though you can find that in heterosexuality too, that self-focus is at the heart of much of homosexuality. The self-focus is a means to finding the missing link that will fix that which is broken inside of you. The definition of healthy heterosexuality is mutuality.

As I eventually realized this, I began longing for true compatibility based on mutuality. This positive sign that I was recognizing the key differences between homosexuality and heterosexuality and moving beyond meeting my selfish needs and into a place where I could *give* in a relationship didn't mean I was close to developing such a relationship.

Often men and women who aren't finished dealing with the root issues that led them to act out homosexually mistakenly think that pursuing heterosexuality can be a simultaneous journey (unless you're already married, and even then to some degree it can't).

Before adding the complexities and responsibilities associated with dating and marriage to your plate, you need to fully experience a healthy period of emotional, physical, and sexual sobriety. Avoid dating pressure while you're making such a significant life change. You don't need it, and the other person doesn't deserve it. Get healthy and then *maybe* pursue a relationship.

My recommendation for dating post-homosexuality is at least two years out. I've met people who successfully moved in that direction way sooner and others who were nowhere near ready to be in heterosexual relationship even six years after being sexually sober. Two years is a nice place to start. And most people who relapse or fall do so within the first year.

No one needs the added pressure of focusing on anything other than holiness and obedience in the early days of change. The second year of pursuing freedom is a time when you are really putting into practice getting your needs met appropriately. While waiting, build on your foundation. Cultivate healthy same-sex friendships that are appropriately intimate. Get grounded in the Bible and in worship and in truth. Learn how to meet your needs in a healthy way so that if and when you do find a godly opposite-sex relationship, it can be a healthy addition to your life.

I began taking steps toward distancing myself from the old and preparing for the new. The mere fact that there was movement in my desires was encouraging. I was becoming dissatisfied with my toxic roommate relationship. During that time I was still torn but actively praying for freedom from my attractions. Freedom was coming and growing.

Around that time I was invited to a gathering with some friends who owned a television station. The invited guest speaker was a Christian leader named Kathy Lechner, a woman best known for her prophetic gift—hearing specific things from the Lord about people she was praying for. During this meeting her goal was to minister to the staff of the television station—people on the front line of Christian ministry. She prayed for people individually out loud and shared a word or picture she felt was from the Lord for each person.

Halfway through this meeting she asked me to stand up. She looked right at me and said a lot of encouraging but challenging things. She noted there was something I had struggled with for many years and that I had prayed for it to be removed. She said, "Today God is taking it from you and answering your prayer."

The first thing that came to my mind was the emotional obsession I had with my roommate. I had struggled with this in other same-sex relationships too. In our ministry we call this emotional dependency. (I recommend reading a booklet by Lori Rentzel called *Emotional Dependency*.) Kathy painted a picture in her words to me of the kind of life the Lord wanted me to have. It was inspiring and not at all spooky. In fact, it was life-giving.

I left that meeting truly feeling free. And from that day on, the very real and ever-present longing I had for my roommate—including the jealousy I experienced when I thought of anyone being near him, the desire to be constantly with him, even the sexual attraction—was gone. I can't explain it other than to say God delivered me.

Please understand that this was years into my journey. And I didn't say God delivered me from other temptations related to my homosexual struggles. God delivered me from this one major area after years of my praying about it. It was amazing, breathtaking, joyous, and unbelievable. Where there had resided an enormous burden and struggle there was now open space for God to fill any way He saw fit.

That began a season of great growth in my life. Where so much of my walk to that point had been pursuing holiness as I *left* the old behind, this new season was marked with pursuing holiness and *walking into* the new. God had been stripping me of the old but was now adding in the new. The season of subtraction was over, and the season of addition—multiplication even—was starting. It was as clearcut as that too.

In this new season, not only did I want a wife and family, but my feelings were beginning to line up with that dream. I'm not saying I was catapulted from one lust to another, or that I had become a skirt chaser, or that I was beginning to objectify women in the way that I had men. God didn't intend for me to think of women the way I'd thought about men—as a means to satisfy my selfish sexual pleasure and immediate needs. He wanted me to see women as *He* sees them. He wanted me to see them as more than my opposite. He wanted me to see them as a complement and as a treasure.

At the same time God was teaching me to see myself as the man He intended me to be. He had made me to be strong, secure, and whole, which has nothing to do with being a womanizer, sports fanatic, or other cultural tests we often use to define manhood.

Meeting Leslie

When I first saw Leslie walk into the living room of the home where

I was attending a church home fellowship group, I remember thinking she was different. She was special. She was mysterious. She was beautiful. Her laugh entranced me. The mystery of who she was engulfed me. I spent all night looking at her, trying to figure out who she was, what her story was, and how I could become her friend. She reminded me of an actress who had once intrigued me. Her curly brown hair and contagious laugh were so attractive. I didn't even know her name, but in my heart and mind we were destined to know each other.

> I believe God was training me like I was preparing for a triathlon. He was walking me through a critical stage of development I'd missed growing up.

While I was definitely growing into my godly masculinity and interested in finding a woman to date, this wasn't an "Oh my gosh, she's hot, and I've got to have her" type of reaction. Instead it was a sincere desire as a man to meet this woman so that we might develop a meaningful friendship. I was aware that whatever was happening to me must happen slowly and deliberately. It was like walking up several flights of stairs, one step at a time, instead of taking the elevator immediately to the top. I wanted to experience each step if God had romance in mind for us.

Sadly, Leslie didn't even notice me that night. Weeks and months rolled by. After seeing her nearly every week at the Bible study and repeated attempts to get her attention through every means I could imagine, she seemed unmoved by my charms. She didn't even look at me. I was sure she was rejecting me, which made me try harder. I wasn't discouraged. I was invigorated. My resolve to know her was galvanized.

Now as I look back at that time (probably around seven months), I believe God was training me like I was preparing for a triathlon. He was walking me through a critical stage of development I'd missed growing up. It was like puberty, part deux.

Very quickly let me explain. I am not a psychologist, but I have done a fair share of studying homosexuality. I have come to see how a disruption or complication experienced during the psychological stages of development common to every human being can contribute to someone developing same-sex attractions. Here's a quick and very general layperson's overview of development stages.

Psychological Stages of Development

At birth until about age 3, we are in a learning phase of understanding through experience that the world is good and all is well. This is when we get our general sense of well-being. The primary caregiver is usually mom, and she meets the child's needs. When the child is hungry, she feeds him. When he's wet or dirty, she cleans him up. When he has a need—whatever the need—mom meets it.

The second stage of development lasts from about age 3.5 years to 6 years. In this phase dad becomes more significant. For boys, dad models sameness. A boy learns what it's like to be the same as dad in every way. Dad shows a boy what masculinity is. For a girl, dad models healthy *difference*. Dad shows a boy how *to be,* and dad shows a girl *how to be treated*. For a boy in this phase, mom learns to let go and allow dad to become the child's guide. Mom isn't replaced in critical areas of nurture, but she is replaced in areas of assimilation as a boy learns to become who dad is.

The third stage of development begins around age 7 and builds on what the child learned in the previous stage. In this peer-driven stage, a boy takes that sameness he learned from dad and develops guy friends who are also the same. Girls start looking at boys as cute and potential mates; boys hate girls because they have cooties. We adults laugh at cooties, but this is a crucial part of a boy's development. A boy, in this phase, is continuing to learn and walk out male "sameness." If puberty is going to go as it should, a boy has to go through that "she has cooties" phase.

The fourth stage of development is puberty. I'm going to focus on boys in this stage. This is the phase where a child becomes attracted to the object of his curiosity, to what is *mysterious* and *different*. For a boy who has successfully come to accept his own maleness, the next conclusion is recognizing that what is different is *female*. Female is different from male. Female is mysterious. Female is what a boy does not understand. This puzzle attracts the boy's attention.

For men who struggle with homosexuality, there has often been a breech somewhere in this developmental process. Most often a boy who struggles with homosexuality has a successful first stage of development. Whether through death, divorce, or lack of connection (actual or perceived), he doesn't go through the second phase successfully or even really enter into it. The old way of talking about this breech is to say, "Homosexual men have overbearing mothers and passive or absent fathers." Yes, that is an oversimplification and doesn't necessarily match every case, but it's not atypical either.

In my case I had a strong mom. (I thank God for her strength.) She taught me things about life and living that have guided my entire life. My dad didn't know how to be a healthy dad because he was an orphan until age 3. His adoptive father died just before my dad turned 10. So Dad had a dad for about six years of his life and during a critical stage of development—but not long enough to teach him what he needed to know. So my dad did what he believed was best: Let women raise the kids while men provide for the physical needs.

Certainly personality plays an enormous role in how we perceive and respond to our environment. As a sensitive kid I perceived that my mom loved me and that my dad didn't. I was grateful that he worked hard and gave us nice things, but when I considered who was always there for me, it was my mom. She became my role model.

For me—and for many of you male readers—there was no second stage of development. The first stage went from birth to age 7. My peers and friends were primarily girls instead of boys. The girls didn't have cooties. They were just like me. I wanted to be one of them. At puberty I became emotionally, physically, and sexually attracted to what was mysterious and different: other boys.

Healing the Stages

When I began my healing process, I didn't need to go back through the first development stage. I had a great mom and my early development was successful. But stage two had to be revisited. And God, using authentic community (Discovery Church and Kirk), helped me understand my sameness through healthy relationships with other men. I learned the lessons God had intended for me to learn as a child with my dad with these godly mentors and peers.

In this critical relearning phase with Kirk, I realized I was male despite my attractions and not possessing many of those key interests "men" typically have (sports and hunting, for example). I learned from Kirk, a safe and spiritually mature father figure, that being a man was *desirable.* I discovered that I could not be excluded from being one for any reason. That was a revelation. Having seen and rejected maleness as modeled by my dad, manhood held no special appeal to me. I hadn't wanted to be a man...until now.

I was solidly in that second stage of redevelopment with Kirk when God did that incredible work of forgiveness in my life with my dad. (See chapter 3.) So Kirk, a much more experienced and healthy father, guided me into godly masculinity and manhood. Also, by this time, my dad was back in my life in a healthy way and becoming a man I wanted to emulate for the first time. God was remaking my dad right before my eyes and healing the brokenness of our past. It was awesome.

God was delivering me from my inner vow that I would never be like my dad...or any man. He knew in that redevelopment phase I needed to find a surrogate father and a spiritual mentor. He also knew I needed to experience the healing firsthand via the transformation I saw in my dad and the restoration of our relationship.

The third stage of redevelopment for me included a couple of things. God had begun helping me learn to relate appropriately to other men. This was during my time at Exchange Ministries. I was in support groups with other men seeking freedom. Again, this is one more example of why I call Exchange a stepping-stone. It was moving from the safety of being in relationship with people broken just like me to going into the church to build relationships with people who didn't have the same struggles I did.

At Discovery Church a group of guys and I became friends. Tom was kind of the leader of the single guys. He was a little older than me, had been divorced, and was a father of two. He was what I would have called a real man. He was typical in his male interests, such as sports, but he was godly and exuded compassionate masculinity. He reached out to me and accepted me. (When he remarried I was one of his groomsmen.) I didn't have a thing in common with him really, but we connected in spite of that. This time of building friendships with men and not only knowing, but feeling, that I was their equal and accepted in their male community for the first time in my life was the ultimate in living out the sameness I had learned from Kirk and my dad. On a very meaningful level, we were the same despite our different interests. The feeling was not unlike finding out I was the *first* one chosen to be on a team.

Back to Leslie

All that to say that at the time I was meeting Leslie at the Bible studies, I was fully entering into heterosexual puberty at age 24. Okay, it was a little late, but not too late for it to work out just fine.

Finally my efforts to get to know Leslie were successful. In July we were invited to go on a three-day deep-sea fishing excursion with ten other home groupers. Leslie and I ended up on the same boat. One early morning while our die-hard fishing friends were looking for a perfect catch, Leslie and I began talking. We talked about everything from how nice it was to be in our warm bunkbeds to how crazy our friends were for fishing all night. We discussed our lives, families, and work.

That fishing trip was the beginning of what I knew would be a great friendship. When we returned to Orlando, Leslie and I became inseparable. We found we were definitely compatible and became one another's closest friend. There were a few times in those early months that I wondered if there was something more going on. I was a little afraid of what it might mean. Commitment always made me a little nervous. (How's *that* for a typical male response?) Yet we continued being great friends...until my feelings were unmistakable. I knew I had fallen for Leslie and that I needed to tell her.

After lunch one Sunday we went for a walk. I shared my feelings. Her response was kind, but firm. She said she loved me too much as a friend to string me along. She also said, "Alan, it's *never* going to happen."

I was jarred but undeterred. In fact, her adamant negative response caused me to pray harder and ask the Lord to give me perspective, patience, and perseverance. And He did.

Months went by with seemingly no change. As Leslie would later describe it, I stepped back but not away. She knew my feelings weren't changing, and so her platonic love for me and her concern for my heart caused her to pray daily that my feelings would change. She wanted our friendship to continue unhindered by inappropriate romantic feelings on my part.

Her prayers had the opposite effect. It wasn't too long after my declaration that I absolutely knew I was in love with her and that she was going to be my wife. I didn't know *how* God was going to swing that, but I knew He had solved bigger problems. He could do this.

When I turned 25 my friends, including Leslie, threw me the perfect surprise party. It was amazing. They paid a local comedy club to turn the second half of their performance into an improvisational skit about my life. It was awesome. I had so much fun! As Leslie, and others who knew her, would later say, she had so much fun watching me have the time of my life.

At the end of the night some friends and I walked Leslie to her car. I thanked her for her part in the surprise with a hug. She told me later that hug caused a few sparks to fly into her heart. She spent the weekend in bed feeling sick and praying that whatever those sparks were they would go away. But they didn't. She knew at the end of that weekend that she not only liked me, she *loved* me—as only a woman can love a man. (I'm smiling!)

A New Relationship

We went on our first real date in March, and I proposed over dinner. It wasn't a traditional proposal with a ring and me on bended knee. I simply said, "So when are we getting married?"

To my extreme surprise she responded, "January third is a Saturday. I've already looked on my calendar." In just a few short hours of dating, we were engaged. While I definitely had butterflies, I knew God had answered my prayers and honored my fight for His—and my—dream!

Wonderful moments are sometimes followed by not-so-wonderful ones. That first date started great, but the reality that Leslie and I had moved from best friends to engaged in one evening freaked me out. My "flight" mechanism kicked into high gear at Leslie's acceptance of my proposal. My insecurities got the better of me. I was terrified. I made it through the evening and dropped Leslie off at her home as quickly as I could. I wanted to get home and go to bed. Maybe the escape of sleep would help me feel better. It didn't. The next day I filled my journal and wrote Leslie letters telling her I had moved too fast. Then I called my best friend for help. I couldn't believe I was feeling so upset about all of this.

I finally called Leslie and told her how afraid I was. I suggested we talk to my counselor (someone who had no connection to the issue of homosexuality, by the way).

I went to see my counselor, and he helped me tremendously. He told me to move slowly and enjoy this new relationship. He helped me understand that commitment issues were common to men in general. I wasn't experiencing a homosexual problem, just a *guy* problem. He helped me get past the distorted view that relationship, commitment, and Leslie were things to be feared. I soon realized that those things were going to be anchors for me. Life relaxed a bit, and Leslie and I continued to date and make plans.

I struggled one more time a couple of months later with the quickening approach of the wedding date. One issue was that we lived in Florida, but she was from California, and she wanted to get married in California. I had agreed but wasn't excited about it. I told Leslie I thought we should postpone our marriage a few months. I will never forget that conversation on her front steps outside of her house.

She looked at me and said, "Postponing isn't an option. You either want to marry me or you don't. I don't care about any of the planning or where we get married. I just want to marry you. Do you want to marry me?"

That night I knew I *did* want to marry her more than anything in the world. Her agreeing to get married anywhere helped me relax.

A New Learning Curve

I share all of this so you can see the battle that was raging and the fear I had. Leslie and I worked through the difficult issues together and separately. It helped us realize who we were and what our weaknesses were. It also taught me a lot about grace. I was so riddled with fear about the details, but Leslie was calm and full of grace and truth. She walked through that time with me without taking my irrational moments personally. I'm amazed when I think of how good and solid and secure she was through all my turmoil. She also allowed me to learn to lead her.

I didn't struggle with worry about getting married after that night. We had five glorious months of planning for our big day. It was a joyous time.

I began asking my guy friends who had overcome homosexuality and gotten married what I should expect on the wedding night. I wasn't about to let *that* send me into a tizzy, but I was a little nervous. I was a heterosexual virgin.

A couple of friends suggested Leslie and I wait until the second night of our honeymoon so we wouldn't be so exhausted after the wedding frenzy. They said to enjoy the newness the first night, get a good night's sleep, and then let nature happen the next night. Another friend even suggested we wait three days.

One night I was at dinner with my friend Victor, the one whose family owns a Christian TV station. While we were at dinner a lady

I'd met at the staff/volunteer gathering Victor invited me to came up to our table. She asked how I was and said that Victor had told her I was engaged. I thought knowing my past and remembering the prophecy I'd been given that night, this lady would marvel at the awesome work God was doing in my life. Maybe she felt that way, but she didn't say so. Instead she looked at me and said, "Remember, Alan, sex doesn't equal intimacy."

A little taken aback I said, "I know."

She said it again with emphasis. "*Sex doesn't equal intimacy.* Never forget that." Both of us reiterated our points. I knew she was saying something profound, and I thanked her for it even though I thought it a bit odd.

Leslie and I were married before 200 of our closest family and friends in the church where I grew up—the same church where I told my mom when I was ten that I wanted to get married. It was the happiest day of my life. Even better than the dream I'd held onto for nearly two decades! I remember walking into the service and through the congregation elated by God's goodness and full of joy at all He'd healed me of and given to me. Seeing Leslie come in and walk toward me was also overwhelming. Our day was perfect.

And just as I knew it would, our first night together arrived. Leslie and I had agreed about enjoying our first night together with no pressure of sex. It was great. We spent the first night at a hotel by the airport because we were flying to Jamaica the next day.

We arrived in Jamaica and then traveled two hours by bus to our hotel. We went through small towns on rough back roads. It was actually a little frightening. By the time we got there it was very late. The bus didn't have air conditioning, and it was hot. All I wanted to do was sleep. But my new wife had planned for our second night to be "the night." We were married. She had waited her whole life for this moment, never giving herself away to another man.

I admit fear came. I hoped the ordeal of our arrival would sway her to wait one more day. I'd even shared the story of my friend who had waited until the third night. Leslie didn't latch on to the idea. That first night in Jamaica was tense. I was scared. She was hurt and feeling undesirable. That caused my old tapes of not measuring up to what a "real man" should be to start playing. We postponed our union and made it through the awkwardness.

That third evening I started worrying even more. Maybe the long wait had caused expectations that also caused stress.

We went to dinner and then came back to our room to get ready for bed.

Everything was going great…

Let me pause right here to say that I'm relating the following because there is a lot to learn from our experience…er…inexperience.

As I said, everything was going great until the time came to put everything where it needs to go…and it…didn't happen. I tried again and got nervous, sure I was doing something wrong, which naturally caused me to focus on my insecurity. The end result was a very ruined moment and tears. *My* tears, not Leslie's.

Thinking back on that night now, I want to help that poor 25-year-old, inexperienced kid.

Leslie, in what had to be a very difficult moment personally, grabbed me and hugged me. She cried with me and prayed for me. She told me she hadn't married me for sex, and that if we *never* had sex she would still love me and cherish being my wife. I was awed by her selflessness…but upset too by my inability to perform.

The next night I was nervous but determined to successfully finish what we'd started the night before. Sounds romantic, eh? We got to that same point, and the same thing happened. It was like I hadn't read the instruction manual. And because she'd never done this either, she didn't have any suggestions. We didn't know it at the time, but we were having a very natural problem.

Because of my previous life, I was so sure I was broken. I experienced severe performance anxiety. This only compounded the problem that was really wholly unrelated to attraction, homosexual struggles, or lack of heterosexual desire for my wife.

Leslie and I talked about our struggles, committed to working through them, and prayed. We also decided to have fun discovering everything we could about one another intimately—what we liked and what we didn't like without con-templating performance. That's when I told Leslie about the lady who had drilled into my head at dinner that sex wasn't equivalent to intimacy.

> We learned how to make the other person feel loved, accepted, and excited.

A light went on! I realized I was trying to "have sex" with my wife...not trying to be intimate with her. While our problem was completely natural, I think God was using our inex-perience to get us to a place of experiencing each other *intimately* without sex. Remember, God hadn't created me to use Leslie the way I had used men in my past. He wanted me to love her, respect her, and make love to her in the way she was created to be loved.

The rest of our honeymoon was all about being with one another intimately. We may not have had sex *technically,* but we were definitely close in a way I had never been with anyone. And we learned how to make the other person feel loved, accepted, and excited. By the end of the week we were enjoying sexual contact and trusting that at some point everything would work out according to God's plan.

The last night in Jamaica, while we were eating dinner, Leslie looked at me and said, "God is writing our story. Someday we will talk about this, laugh about this, and help others struggling with the same thing."

One night at a ladies Bible study about two weeks after we'd gotten married, a friend of ours pulled Leslie aside and asked her what was wrong. Leslie didn't think she was giving off any weird vibes, but this woman could tell something wasn't quite going well. Leslie shared that we hadn't technically gotten the whole sex thing to work yet. Our friend laughed and said that it had taken her and her husband six weeks to figure it out when they got married because they were both virgins and just couldn't get how it all worked. Leslie came home on cloud nine, laughing and thrilled. She was sure such news would really encourage me, especially because the man in the story hadn't come from a gay background.

I was flawed, I realized, *but more normal than I imagined.*

Eventually our sexual issue was resolved. And what I had been told by that woman months earlier was exactly right: Sex does not equal intimacy. Although there were some rough nights for us wondering what in the world was wrong, even in those understandable moments of frustration we had time to get to know one another and time to experience real intimacy.

The night we finally got it right was very fulfilling for both of us. We laughed and cried and held each other for hours in awe. It was *so* worth the wait.

As we laughed and talked about it, we couldn't imagine how people less mature than us, especially middle and high school students, could handle such an enormous issue as sex. How could people do this with just anyone? How could they do it without knowing the first thing about real intimacy? So much went through our heads and hearts as we experienced the miraculous way God intended for us to experience it.

And now here I am, typing this chapter without shame or fear, completely on the other side of the issue hoping you too will have the joy God can bring to relationships.

Is Marriage for You?

As we've discussed, the primary goal isn't heterosexuality, it's holiness. And neither should your goal be marriage. Truly God brought Leslie and me together. For some women and men who leave the homosexual life, marriage will be an eventual result. But not for everyone. As you walk through the healing process, wait and watch. Look forward in anticipation to what God will do. Surely your desires will be part of His equation. If you strongly desire a family, God knows that. And, in time, He may bring it to pass.

With Leslie and me, and with other couples I know who have come out of homosexuality (both gay men and lesbians), the road to marriage doesn't usually start with sexual attraction. More likely it will start as a God-directed friendship. Over time, that friendship may lead to a strong emotional (again, not sexual) attraction. And with the passage of more time, that strong emotional attraction may lead to an emotional and spiritual commitment culminating in marriage. In marriage, the sexual component will happen. For some, it will happen right away with no problems. With others, it may be more like Leslie and me— time and intimacy having their desirable results.

Part 3

Special
Considerations

When You're Leaving Lesbianism
by Yvette Schneider

A Note from Alan

I've asked my friend and colleague Yvette Schneider to add a chapter relating to the special aspects of leaving homosexuality from a lesbian viewpoint. You'll find her insights and story very helpful and interesting.

Leaving Lesbianism

When I made the decision to leave my lesbian lifestyle, it wasn't to become heterosexual. I didn't want to be heterosexual. In fact, the thought of dating or marrying a man was abhorrent. My motivation for walking away from the only truly intimate and connected relationships I'd ever known was to live in obedience to Christ.

I went from being a radical, anti-Christian lesbian activist to being a radical lover of Jesus. The thrill of a new life in Christ with its endless possibilities through a genuine relationship with the King of kings and Lord of lords was all I wanted. Whatever it took to live in obedience to Jesus, I was willing to do.

Having a rush of emotion when you first accept Jesus as Lord and Savior is normal. In the excitement I was willing to do anything He asked of me. Every free moment I had, I spent reading my Bible. I memorized scripture during my lunch break. I prayed and waited expectantly to hear the still, small voice of God in my heart.

When I read Romans 1:21,26-27 during my first week as a Christian, I knew instantly that I could not continue to live as a lesbian:

> Although they knew God, they neither glorified him as God nor gave thanks to him…Because of this, God gave them over to shameful lusts. Even their women exchanged natural relations for unnatural ones. In the same way the men also abandoned natural relations with women and were inflamed with lust for one another. Men committed indecent acts with other men, and received in themselves the due penalty for their perversion.

But the emotional high I experienced when I committed my life to Jesus didn't last long. What followed was loneliness, despair, and an extended stay in my loving God's refining fire.

In the midst of my pain, I had a decision to make. Would I follow God and pursue holiness even if that meant I would be alone and struggling with same-sex attractions for the rest of my life? Or would I make excuses to justify living according to my fleshly desires? Would I only serve God if I knew, beyond a shadow of a doubt, that He would remove my lesbian attractions? Was my motivation to pursue God or to seek my own comfort?

A holy life would require abstaining from lesbian sexual relationships and idolatrous relationships. That meant avoiding relationships in which I looked to another woman to meet my emotional needs (also known as emotional dependency). What is an emotionally dependent relationship? It's when your thoughts are always centered on your friend. You wonder what she's thinking about you, and you plan conversations with her in your head. You're jealous of your friend's other friends. You may begin losing interest in other friendships, desiring to only spend time alone with your special friend. If your friend doesn't spend enough time with you, you may feel insecure, angry, or depressed.

My leaving lesbianism required setting aside lesbian and emotionally dependent relationships—everything I used for support up to that point.

There are several people in the Bible who sacrificed everything for God. They didn't hold back, hoping to strike a bargain with a genie-like God. They didn't say, "I'll serve you *if* You promise to grant me my wishes." I turned to them for inspiration.

Shadrach, Meshach, and Abed-nego were thrown by Nebuchadnezzar into a fiery furnace for not bowing down to worship a golden idol the king had set up. They knew the consequence of their refusal was death, but they firmly declared, "If it be so, our God whom we serve is able to deliver us from the furnace of blazing fire; and He will deliver us out of your hand, O king. But even if He does not, let it be known to you, O king, that we are not going to serve your gods or worship the golden image that you have set up" (Daniel 3:17-18 NASB).

Job, while enduring the death of his children, the loss of his wealth, and the affliction of painful boils, said, "Though He slay me, I will hope in Him" (Job 13:15 NASB).

Queen Esther, when faced with the prospect of execution for approaching the king uninvited to plead for lives of the Jews, said, "If I perish, I perish" (Esther 4:16).

It would have been easy for any of these people to say, "Forget God. I'm going to save myself." (The one exception is Job, who couldn't have saved himself from the agony meted out to him by Satan, but he could have followed the advice of his wife to "curse God and die.")

Overcoming sinful behaviors and temptations is much the same as the trials these heroes of faith faced. Like them, reliance on God is our only hope in overcoming. But this reliance can only happen if we trust God. Trust is developed through a strong relationship with Him that allows the Holy Spirit to work in our lives.

Feelings and patterns of behavior that are ingrained (like same-sex attractions) are not going to diminish without the help of the Holy Spirit. But the good news is that the Bible says change for people with same-sex attractions is possible. Some of us used to be gay-identified, but we aren't anymore. We have been washed, sanctified, and justified, just as were the former homosexuals in the early church (1 Corinthians 6:9-11).

Although we may feel overwhelmed by our lesbian feelings and emotional dependencies, and for that reason are turning our lives over to Christ, it's a mistake to make overcoming lesbianism our primary goal.

The Bible says that we must love God with all of our hearts, minds, souls, and strength. Our primary focus should always be to know and love God more as we grow in Him. A strong relationship with God is the foundation for overcoming same-sex attractions.

Leaving Lesbianism Is Difficult

At times, leaving the lesbian life can seem like attempting to swim from Los Angeles to Waikiki. Impossible, suicidal, and just plain crazy. You're working on changing thinking patterns and behaviors that have been part of your life for a very long time, and chances are you won't see dramatic results overnight. For me the changes in my relationships, behaviors, thought processes, and attitudes took years. Most of the time I felt as if I were taking two steps forward and one step back.

Those years were filled with frustration and discouragement, but also with intervals of intense connection with God and unfathomable joy and peace. Obviously it was worth it. I'm still here—serving God and loving my life in Christ.

Expectations

Because of the difficulties, it's important to have realistic expectations during this process of change. Significant change must necessarily take place slowly. Your head would explode if everything about you that needed to change happened all at once. You would be unrecognizable to yourself and to those around you.

God doesn't force change upon us; that isn't the way He works. Be patient. Give yourself a break as you go along. Don't beat yourself up over every misstep and failure.

The Bible says that a righteous person falls seven times and gets back up. Your responsibility following a fall is to get up again, continue on your journey, and not give up because you're not perfect. It doesn't matter whether the fall was a sexual fall or fantasizing about an emotionally dependent relationship with a "special friend."

The apostle Paul says in his letter to the Romans that there is no condemnation for those who are in Christ Jesus. And if you have accepted Christ, you are *in* Him. So don't punish yourself for making mistakes. The Holy Spirit will gently show you when you've missed the mark and need to get back on track. That's the difference between condemnation and what is called "conviction." Condemnation *punishes;* conviction *corrects.* Being "correctable" is one of the most important character traits we can develop.

> Being correctable is one of the most important character traits we can develop...This means when we need to change, we are willing to change.

Years ago one of my pastors said he prayed daily for God to make him "humble, teachable, and correctable." I too began praying for those qualities...with a special emphasis on being "correctable." Being correctable means when we need to change, we are willing to change.

When correction comes from an authority figure, from a friend, or from an accountability partner, it's easy to be offended. But when we focus on the perceived offense, we miss the opportunity for constructive criticism to lead to spiritual growth.

For years I had to tell myself, "Correction is not rejection." Just because someone corrects us doesn't mean she is rejecting us. It's the exact opposite! A true friend will risk upsetting us for our benefit. The Bible says, "Faithful are the wounds of a friend, but deceitful are the kisses of an enemy" (Proverbs 27:6 NASB). We need correction and insight from trusted friends and counselors because we're often too close to our own lives to determine what areas need to change. We only know we don't want to be enslaved to homosexual lust and relational idolatry. But those are really symptoms of deeper issues.

How do we identify those deeper issues? How do we know what other areas of our lives need to change? How do we listen to and remember what God has spoken to us in our hearts and through His Word?

One way for me was to journal. This became essential to my journey out of lesbianism. I found it helpful to write down my thoughts and emotions as they were happening. I didn't try to analyze or censor them. I just wrote them down as they came.

Some women, especially those raised in Christian homes, feel guilty expressing negative thoughts and emotions. But the Bible says God wants us to be truthful about what is in our hearts (Psalm 51:6). He already knows our hearts anyway; we're not going to surprise Him. I have stacks of notebooks I've used for journaling over the years. I told my husband and sister that when I die, they need to destroy them immediately. Those journals are filled with years and years of hopes and dreams, revelations about God and me, milestones, and spiritual breakthroughs. But most of those journals also contain page after page of confessions, bad attitudes, obsessions, jealousies, offenses by others, and a myriad of complaints. In these journals I vented to God. I would tell Him honestly how I felt almost daily.

Journaling helped me connect with my feelings, especially those I refused to show others. If someone hurt my feelings, I covered it up. I didn't want anyone to think they had the power to hurt me. I was an expert at outwardly masking my inner responses to hurts and slights. My friend and one-time roommate Tami amazed me. She would confront anyone who hurt her in even the smallest way. I couldn't understand how she allowed herself to be unguarded or why she would want to be vulnerable. In my world, vulnerability was not an asset. It was a detriment of massive proportions. But through journaling I could explore being vulnerable to God.

Journaling also allowed me to identify my "trigger people." Trigger people are those women who have qualities that draw us to them like a magnet. For me, it was women who were emotionally unavailable, competent in their work, involved in their own lives (not needy), and attractive to other people (not necessarily in the physical sense, but in personality or demeanor).

Women who identify as lesbian or who have same-sex attractions are not attracted to all women—only certain women or certain types of women. It's important for a woman leaving lesbianism to identify what characteristics in another woman attract her, what qualities "trigger" her attraction. The qualities I found attractive were very specific. And after months of journaling, I learned them and how they compared to the qualities of friends I liked but felt no sexual attraction or desire to bond with as "special friends."

Once we know what types of women trigger us, we can wisely stay away from them as much as possible. Especially avoiding one-on-one situations is prudent when we're first emerging from lesbian life. This gives us a chance to decompress, to find out who we are in Christ, and to discover God's radical love for us without needless distractions. Beyond that, spending time away from women who trigger us gives us time to build friendships with women who don't.

Many women who struggle with same-sex attractions are currently involved in an emotionally dependent relationship that may or may not be sexual. It's common for women in these types of relationships to justify maintaining them by saying, "I can't abandon the friendship. That wouldn't be loving. After all, I'm not going to treat her the way I don't want to be treated." Or, "We're not having sex; we're just good friends."

There are times when a woman is emotionally and psychologically unable to end an emotionally dependent relationship without severe consequences, including suicidal thoughts. Relationships that have served as the primary source of a woman's love and affection can be akin to a lifeline. If abruptly ended, this lifeline would also be severed. If you have suicidal thoughts after ending a lesbian relationship, contact a therapist or counselor immediately. It is important, however, to end inappropriate and sinful relationships.

Think about a married woman emotionally involved with another man. Her only option as a Bible-believing Christian is to cut-off that extra-marital relationship at once. Continuing contact with the other man would perpetuate an inappropriate relationship. The same is true of lesbian relationships.

We need to avoid making excuses for keeping our emotionally dependent relationships alive. The longer we drag out an unhealthy relationship, the longer it will take to be truly free of same-sex attractions and emotional dependencies.

We can be reassured during this difficult time in our lives that God will never give us more than we're able to handle: "No temptation has overtaken you but such as is common to man; and God is faithful, who will not allow you to be tempted beyond what you are able, but with the temptation will provide the way of escape also, so that you will be able to endure it" (1 Corinthians 10:13 NASB).

When I was a new Christian, I didn't know how to avoid becoming emotionally dependent on another woman. I had never heard the term "emotional dependency." I thought I was just someone who connected quickly and intensely with other people. As a result, I was unaware of my tendency to home in on women who possessed my trigger attributes.

In an early conversation on my journey out of lesbianism I bemoaned the fact that my local friends had abandoned me and I was now friendless. The woman who was discipling me encouraged me to call at least two young women in the church whom I thought would make good friends and reach out to them. After all, friends are those who show themselves friendly.

You can guess how that turned out.

I became emotionally dependent on one of them almost immediately, which began a three-year struggle (and I mean struggle) to overcome my idolatrous attachment to her. I didn't know that I was walking into a trap when I befriended Michelle. Only as I learned about the emotional dependency aspect of lesbianism did I realize I was attaching myself to her in an unhealthy manner.

That is when I should have walked away from the friendship. But I didn't. I lied to myself about the nature of my feelings for her. This prolonged the agonizing relationship that resulted in years of heartache.

As women overcoming lesbianism, it's imperative that we be honest with ourselves about our feelings for women who may trigger us. After learning what characteristics trigger you, make it a habit to notice when someone is triggering you and avoid contact with her. The Bible says to "flee from youthful lusts" (2 Timothy 2:22 NASB) and to "flee from idolatry" (1 Corinthians 10:14 NASB). Whether you're a youth or not, escaping a situation that may cause you to stumble is always the best policy.

The potential downside of avoiding someone to not develop an unhealthy attachment or when we're trying to overcome an unhealthy attachment, is the tendency to isolate. Many women overcoming same-sex attractions tend to hole-up and wall-off to a greater degree than most people experiencing difficult times in their lives. It takes a lot of energy to be around people. We need to pull ourselves out of our malaise and put on a pleasant demeanor. When we're around other people, we need to be good listeners and let other people talk about their lives. We put our problems aside. Connecting this way with other people is exactly what we need to do to get "out of our heads" for a while.

When I was emotionally dependent on a woman, all of my thoughts were consumed with her. I eventually realized that those thoughts were all conversations I was imagining having with the woman in question. The interesting aspect of these internal conversations was that they were all about me. I would talk about myself endlessly, portraying myself in the best light possible. I would imagine the responses I hoped to elicit from her or how I could get her to like me more or be more dependent on me. The conversations in my head were truly "all about me," and how I could get *my* needs met through this woman. Finding ways to stop thinking about myself and start thinking about other people by spending time with them and relating socially to them was one of the most important factors in my healing. Perhaps that will be true of you as well.

At the root of our thoughts and fantasies about women are deep-seated, unmet needs for love, affection, acceptance, and approval. Simply denying these needs by focusing on others will help decrease our self-obsession, but it won't help us actually meet those still unmet legitimate needs. Needs designed by God are met by Him alone. Intimate time spent with the Lord—our Father who loves us more than we can understand—will begin to touch that part of our hearts that we've guarded because of fear of hurt and rejection.

While there is a need deep within us that can only be met by God, God has also created a need in us for human relationship. That need is designed to be met by healthy relationships in the church—the body of Christ. Paul, in a letter to the Corinthians, likens the church to a human body, where each part of the body has a necessary function in order for the rest of the body to function properly.

> God will use the circumstances of your life to draw you closer to Him and to bring healing and wholeness to your life.

We were created as relational beings. God confirmed this when He told Adam that it was not good for him to be alone, even though Adam spent each day walking in the Garden of Eden with God. It is important for us to find people we can bond with through small group situations like those within a good church. Some churches have small groups that meet in people's homes or at the church. Others have groups that meet to study the Bible or have sharing groups exclusively for women and for men. In this setting we can build friendships with women (and men) who will pray for us and love us as sisters in the Lord.

Many women who have overcome lesbianism say that married couples at church who befriended them and invited them into their homes for regular fellowship gave them some of the most healing experiences of their lifetimes. Spending time with married couples allows us to see how men and women relate to each other. It allows us to feel the comfort and love of a family that can touch a part of our hearts that desperately needs to feel loved and accepted.

(If you don't have the opportunity to spend time with a godly married couple, don't be discouraged. I never had that opportunity, yet God brought me exactly what I needed in my journey out of lesbianism.

He will do the same for you. God will never fail you or forsake you. To do so would violate His character and His promises.)

Whatever our situations, God will use the circumstances of our lives to draw us closer to Him and to bring us healing and wholeness. In fact, "God causes *all things* to work together for good to those who love God, to those who are called according to His purpose" (Romans 8:28 NASB).

When we have successfully navigated our trials, we will be fit to strengthen those who are struggling with similar trials. We won't develop true compassion and love for others if we don't endure hardships or if our faith is never tested and strengthened.

The apostle Paul writes to the church in Corinth, "Blessed be the God and Father of our Lord Jesus Christ, the Father of mercies and God of all comfort, who comforts us in all our affliction so that we will be able to comfort those who are in any affliction with the comfort with which we ourselves are comforted by God" (2 Corinthians 1:3-4 NASB).

You may not care at this point that your trials will be used to comfort others in their future trials. I was told while in the throes of a torturous emotional dependency that one day God would use my experiences to help others. I remember thinking, *Who cares? That doesn't help me now.* But in the months that followed, it helped to know that the trials I was enduring were not in vain. I was growing increasingly closer to God and developing a greater love for others that would one day indeed be used by God for His purposes.

Today I often meet women who are single-minded in their quest to abolish their same-sex attractions. I tell them it's also important to focus on aspects of life that are not directly related to homosexuality. Homosexuality is not the biggest issue in our lives (our relationship with God is). Changing any aspect of our lives that affects the way we think and respond will produce a measure of change in our same-sex attractions.

One of the first issues I had to deal with when I became a Christian and left the lesbian lifestyle was my relationship with authority. I was utterly unwilling to trust anyone in authority, especially women. My mom was the primary authority in my life. (God bless her. She wasn't a Christian when I was growing up, but she is now a strong one who talks about Jesus with every person she meets.) My dad was distant and uninvolved. Draconian is the only way to describe my mom's style of discipline. There was no reward for being honest. Punishment in my house was swift and arbitrary. As a result, lying became almost second nature to me. It was the only way to escape severe consequences.

Many women who struggle with same-sex attractions have the opposite experience with their mothers. Their mothers may have been weak and their fathers intolerant, authoritative, and abusive. Sexual abuse is common among women with same-sex attractions. Other behaviors that result in childhood emotional scarring are often prevalent. The result is the same: distrust of authority.

I could never bring myself to trust the woman at church who was supposed to be the primary authority in my life. She was my discipler, the woman who would help me develop a strong relationship with Jesus. Only I saw her as someone who would likely mete out punishment of some sort if I admitted that my ongoing struggle with same-sex attractions wasn't improving. I was convinced that if the people in authority were aware of the intensity of my struggles, they would excommunicate me.

For years there was no discernible change in my same-sex attractions. They didn't diminish one iota. Plus, as mentioned, I became emotionally dependent on one of my friends at church. My discipler, Suzanne, knew it. In fact, she's the one who confronted me about the nature of that relationship. She said, "Yvette, you have an inappropriate relationship with Michelle. You're jockeying for position to be number one in her life, and you'll do anything to make sure you keep that spot."

If I had been honest with Suzanne over the years and admitted that I continued to struggle with my desire to be "number one" in Michelle's life, I believe the intense and sometimes overwhelming feelings I had to possess Michelle would have waned much sooner than they did. But I hid those feelings from Suzanne. And my relationship with her was strained. She always knew I was hiding information, and I always knew she knew.

This is a perfect example of how not to behave with authority. If you have a problem confiding in an authority figure, be honest about it. A person of integrity will either help you work through your fears or will refer you to someone who is better able to relate to you. Look for someone, whether it is a professional counselor, pastoral counselor, or lay leader, who is willing to walk alongside you in your journey out of lesbianism with an attitude of love and kindness, with a strong sense of boundaries, and with a commitment to challenge attitudes, beliefs, and behaviors that are inhibiting your spiritual growth and your relationships with others.

I was not honest with, nor did I trust, people in authority. That wasn't good at all.

Developing Friendships

When I first became a Christian, I lived with several young Christian women. That allowed me to develop healthy friendships with women who became trusted key people in my life. I wasn't attracted to any of them, nor were any of the other young women who eventually became my closest friends trigger people. This was during the time that I was also emotionally involved with Michelle. All I wanted to do when I got home from work was to hole up and read my Bible. But living with several roommates made isolation impossible. I forced myself to befriend women I had no interest in whatsoever. I didn't know how to talk to them or relate to them. It wasn't exciting for me at all. But I knew I needed to healthily connect with women who didn't share my struggles.

Since we all lived in the same house together, I had to learn how to confront my roommates with grievances and how to handle conflicts appropriately. We all loved the Lord and wanted to live for Him as best we could, so we were motivated to learn how to handle negative situations in the best way possible. An oft-quoted scripture in our house was "Iron sharpens iron, so one man sharpens another" (Proverbs 27:17 NASB).

I had to learn how to be vulnerable with my friends, to share my hopes and dreams...and also my struggles, shortcomings, fears, and vulnerabilities. It was difficult to trust that they wouldn't use that information against me in some way. But that's the nature of friendship! To step out and take a risk for the sake of truly knowing another person. I had to allow myself to be known, even if that meant sharing details I was ashamed of or embarrassed

> The road to healthy friendships isn't an easy one. Friendships may be hard for you, but they are vital.

by. That was the only way people could truly know me. The result was that I forged close friendships with women I would never have imagined would be my friends. I look back on that time in my life with fondness. I know the strength of my friendships that were second only to my relationship with God helped me through the dark times of overcoming same-sex attractions.

My friend Sally loved me for who I was even though we were very different. She loved to shop and was very friendly and animated. Carrie pursued me when I would isolate (she still does). Loriene had a homosexual background, but it was her tolerance, insight, and willingness to challenge me that solidified our friendship.

Making room in your life for friends who are different from you will help you tremendously as you pull out of unhealthy habits.

The road to healthy friendships isn't an easy one. My friends hurt my feelings and let me down frequently. I learned over time not to have unrealistic expectations of others and not to be easily offended. Friendships may be hard for you, but they are vital.

Are you thinking, *Well it's easy to build friendships with people when they're roommates?* Not all of my friends were my roommates. In fact, three of my bridesmaids were never my roommates. I also have many other friends that I've made over the years as I've moved from city to city with my family. I learned that in order to make new friends in a healthy way, it's important to learn the social art of small talk.

Many women involved in lesbian relationships and emotional dependencies find little use for small talk. It may even be an entirely unknown form of social interaction to them. I know it was for me. Unless I could talk to someone about deep things, I wasn't interested in a friendship. If I were going to make new friends, I had to learn how to not jump to personal intimacy—to let it develop slowly.

In my early years as a Christian, I spent a lot of time around other women, observing them interact with one another. How did they communicate with new people? What did they talk about? How did they keep conversations going? As much as I didn't like to shop (a favorite activity among my straight friends), I knew I had to join other women in doing things they liked to do. It's so important not to limit ourselves by adopting the attitude that because we don't like to do something, we're not going to do it. I'm not saying we have to go shopping and try on slinky cocktail dresses or have our makeup done in the middle of a department store. But we can go shopping with some friends just to be with them. We can observe what women talk about when they're together. We'll probably find that we have more in common than we thought. That doesn't mean that if we like watching or playing sports we have to stop doing those things. I love sports, and I'm not ashamed of that. I also know that to build friendships with some women, I'm going to have to participate in activities they enjoy.

Not only does shopping together give us time to get to know our friends better, it's also a good way to see what kinds of clothes women are wearing. Some women with lesbian pasts have become entrenched in wearing asexual clothing. For some, it's out of opposition to the feminine, for others it is a defensive measure against attracting men, and for yet others it's the result of negative body images.

When we reach a certain level of comfort with our femininity, it's a good idea to observe women our size and build to see what style of clothes they're wearing. Figure out what clothing styles you like, what you're comfortable wearing, and what complements your body type.

Wearing more feminine clothing will also help you to *feel* more feminine, and as you feel more feminine, you will want to embrace more feminine clothing, makeup, and hairstyles. *A change in your outward appearance is not a prerequisite for overcoming lesbianism.* It's only a continuation of the changes the Holy Spirit is making in your heart.

Women leaving lesbianism are prone to self-absorption. We can easily get caught up in our needs, our pain, our struggle. So we need to be aware of other people and their feelings. I felt so ugly physically and in my personality that I didn't think anyone could truly like me, so I didn't think I could hurt someone by withdrawing. But other women have similar hurts, worries, and insecurities. They will miss us when we're gone, and they're going to be hurt if we pull away.

Tami, my ultratransparent friend who always says when something is bothering her, once yelled at me at church because I hadn't asked her if she needed a ride. She proceeded to ride home with me so she could continue airing her grievance about how thoughtless I'd been. I was stunned that I had the power to hurt her. Aside from being yelled at, I felt good that what I did *mattered* to someone. And unfortunately it wasn't the only time I hurt a friend by failing to consider her feelings...and it won't be the last.

There is also a tendency among many women leaving lesbianism toward internalized misogyny. By the time I was a young teen, I had hostile feelings toward my mother. The day I left for college, I leaned out my friend's car window and said, "Your reign of terror is over!" Some women who view their mothers as weak carry that over to all females. Or, as in my case, femaleness is seen as abusive and undesirable.

Still, being female, we need to bond with girls and women in our developmental stages to eventually develop into stable women ourselves. When this doesn't happen, we look to our same sex to complete what is lacking *within* us. We are women, yet inside us we have cut off from other women. We then attempt to become the women we wish we were by connecting emotionally and sexually with other women who possess the qualities we want or who will embrace us the way we wish our mothers had. What we're left with instead of love and appreciation for women is an internalized hatred of our idea of women or of the feminine. Women were too loathsome or weak or unavailable to connect with when we were girls.

That image of the feminine remains within us even as same-sex attractions emerge and we involve ourselves in lesbian relationships. What we need to do is recognize those feelings in ourselves, ask God for forgiveness for our negative views of women, and discover the nature of true femininity. Remember, God created woman!

One way to recognize misogynistic attitudes is to spend time writing in our journals how we felt about our mothers when we were growing up. We can write also about what we think about women who represent, in our opinion, the typical woman: what we think a woman should be, how she should act, how she should dress, how she should relate to others. Not only will this bring out any negative attitudes toward women we may have, it will also reveal areas in our lives where we don't feel we measure up as women.

> As women overcoming same-sex attractions, we need to discover the true feminine and learn to embrace it in ourselves.

As women overcoming same-sex attractions, we need to discover the true feminine and learn to embrace it in ourselves. We probably have distorted views of femininity. I know I did. It's likely that many women aren't aware of what constitutes a godly woman. Our society has become so confused about the true nature of femininity and masculinity that women and men are degraded by the almost comical caricatures of female and male. Men are portrayed as sex-obsessed playboys or beer-guzzling sports fanatics. Women are seen as loose, superficial, and shot full of Botox, silicone, and collagen.

To find the definition of true femininity, forget the magazines in the supermarket check-out lines. Look instead at the woman described in Proverbs 31 of the Bible. This woman is not weak in any way. In fact, the Bible says she "girds herself with strength and makes her arms strong" (Proverbs 31:17 NASB). She doesn't cower in the presence of her husband. Instead, her husband honors the great woman he is blessed to have as a wife. She demonstrates leadership skills within her household and in the outside world. She is a successful businesswoman. She is shrewd as she negotiates for goods in the marketplace. She buys and cultivates land. She is skilled at working with her hands. She is not dominating or tyrannical. She is also not defined by her physical appearance, her makeup, her clothing, or her age.

Many women who struggle with lesbianism have issues with their body image, as do most women in general. No one has the perfect body or the perfect face, not even women who are paid to use their bodies and faces for advertising products. I've read magazine interviews with models and Hollywood A-listers who complain about self-perceived flaws in their appearance. We all have different body types just like we have different personality types, different interests, and different hobbies. Our acceptance of our bodies is reflective of our acceptance of ourselves. When we learn to love and accept ourselves, we will accept our physical appearance.

From the time I was a preteen, I wouldn't look at myself in the mirror unless the light in the bathroom was off. I would open the door just a crack to let a trickle of light stream in from the hallway. It would be just enough light to allow me to see only as much as I needed to see as I brushed my hair and got ready for school. This habit lasted into adulthood. It wasn't until I was well into my thirties and married that I gradually began looking at myself in the mirror with the bathroom light on. My husband helped me accept my physical appearance by his verbal appreciation for how I looked. But self-acceptance wasn't just because another person appreciated my physical appearance. It came through the process of learning week by week, month by month, and year by year to accept myself as a person.

It's common for women leaving lesbianism to go through significant periods of self-pity. This is true of anyone dealing with difficult circumstances in their lives and is often the result of loneliness and sorrow.

Feeling Alone

As a young Christian, I looked at the people around me and felt sorry for myself. We would get together for group activities, and everyone else would play games, laugh, and enjoy each other's company. But I was too self-conscious to participate. I hated party games. Not all games, just those that had a high potential for embarrassing me, such as Charades and Taboo.

And it wasn't only that I didn't fit in with other people that made me feel bad. I also felt my trials were more difficult than theirs. I had more to overcome than they did, and it wasn't fair. Why couldn't I have close friends and struggle with heterosexual lust or consumerism or longing for a husband? Why did my struggle make me such a misfit?

Feeling sad and lonely and out of place is a normal part of leaving lesbianism. We are leaving relationships that fulfilled our need for connection to go into a world in which we may not immediately find relational connections that satisfy.

The upside is that loneliness is our opportunity to grow closer to Jesus. Although the pain of loneliness and despair is the greatest pain we'll probably face on our journey out of lesbianism, it provides a unique opportunity to be intensely connected to God.

I remember going through a particularly difficult few months when I first accepted Jesus as Lord and Savior. My old friends were gone, and I didn't have any new friends yet. I was just learning about God, so I didn't have a strong theological foundation or experience depending on the guidance and grace of God. During this time, someone lent me a tape of a Focus on the Family broadcast featuring a missionary who had been captured as a spy and tortured by the Japanese during World War II.

The heart-wrenching story was that of Darlene Rose, who withstood sickness, starvation, torture, the death of her husband, and the loss of every personal possession she owned for the sake of following Jesus and sharing the good news of the gospel. I listened to that tape over and over to help me understand the depth of someone's commitment to Christ that found physical and emotional hardships tolerable for Jesus Christ. This story and others like it helped me put my struggle into perspective and embrace sorrow and loneliness for the sake of growing closer to Jesus.

Fellowship and Prayer

Some women, when undergoing trials, begin to revise their ideas about God. A common temptation is to develop a new theology. After years of believing that God's Word is clear concerning same-sex relations, you may feel drawn sexually to a woman, and those desires fail to diminish even after months of praying. In a time of intense temptation and weakness, exhausted from willfully resisting sexual contact, you might decide the Bible doesn't really say what you know it says.

Eve faced a similar temptation. The Bible says that when she realized the fruit was good to eat, she ate it. She was tempted by the desire for the knowledge of good and evil so she could be like God, but also by the fruit itself that was good to eat. In that moment of weakness and temptation, Eve falls prey to the enemy's bait: "Has God said…" She then questions God's words, subsequently disregarding them. We are faced with the same struggle as Eve.

Service

A good way to get out of yourself for a while and stop thinking about your problems is to find a place in your church or in your community where you can serve others. This may be vacuuming the church after service, dispensing food in a local soup kitchen or homeless shelter, or joining a group of people in your church for weekend evangelism. Find opportunities that involve helping others. Jesus says that as we feed the hungry, visit the sick, and clothe the naked, we are doing these things to Him (Matthew 25:35-40).

Pain Relief

When we are in pain, our instinctive response is to find a way to end it. Many women who contact me for help expect a formula that will quickly release them from same-sex attractions and relieve their pain. Such a formula does not exist.

If God is the eternal King of kings (and He is), then He is the best one to approach with our requests for help and pain relief. Prayer is our main avenue of communicating with God. The Bible urges us to come to Him often in prayer, to cry before the Lord, to share our hearts with Him, and to ask Him to meet our needs. Our prayers always reach God!

Praying Together

Prayer isn't always a solitary practice. As individual members of the body of Christ, we can ask other people to pray with us. This is where home groups can come into the picture. If there is not an Exodus-member ministry for you to join in your area, look for a church that has people who are accustomed to praying and interceding for others. Intercessors, pastoral counselors, and others know how to pray with someone to ask for forgiveness, to lay aside every encumbrance and sin that so easily entangles, and to loosen the bonds of wickedness. People praying with you is a powerful experience that can have lasting effects.

I remember when my discipler Suzanne said, "I saw a spirit of homosexuality on you."

What? There's something on me? Where?

What she meant was that as she prayed for me, the Holy Spirit revealed to her the spiritual struggle I was engaged in. But why would God reveal something so personal to someone else?

Suzanne wasn't given this information to gossip about me or to ridicule me. The Holy Spirit entrusted her with the information that I needed help in the area of homosexuality because Suzanne was to be one of the primary people helping me. And most of all God knew she would pray for me. And she did—a lot!

I prayed with Suzanne when I forgave my parents for their shortcomings that negatively affected me. Suzanne prayed with me to break any bonds from previous sexual relationships. She spoke words of God's forgiveness over me. She reminded me that if I repented, God was faithful and just to forgive. These words were healing to my soul.

As women, we're drawn to close relationships with other women to a much greater degree than men are to men. We *need* to be in relationship. Not just for fellowship and connection, but for the purpose of approaching the throne of God in prayer for each other.

You will feel a sense of relief and joy after you and/or someone prays for you to be released from the chains that bind you in the spiritual realm. "Our struggle is not against flesh and blood, but against the rulers, against the powers, against the world forces of this darkness, against the spiritual forces of wickedness in the heavenly places" (Ephesians 6:12 NASB).

This doesn't mean you're going to be prayed for once and never struggle again. We are continually being transformed into the image of Christ. This transformation lasts a lifetime. For the rest of our lives, our characters will be molded and changed to come closer to Jesus'. We will be tempted by various forms of sin for as long as we live. None of us will be perfect until we meet Jesus face-to-face. Prayer is one crucial element to living in the freedom Christ gives us.

Worshiping God is central to who we are as children of God. The first time I went to church, I could feel the presence of God so strongly I had to sit throughout the congregation's time of worship. Every Sunday for the next three months, I wept as we worshiped God together. Nothing, outside of Communion, brings the body of Christ together as powerfully as singing worshipful songs together. If you are disconnected from others, joining together in worship is the first step to feeling as if you are part of the greater body of Christ (which you are).

Praying and Worshiping Alone

I encourage you to also worship God when you're alone. I took long drives along Mulholland Drive in Los Angeles and sometimes along the Pacific Coast Highway in Santa Monica and Malibu while playing worship CDs and singing passionately. I chose songs that represented what I needed to know about God's character, His love for me, His faithfulness, and His majesty. I listened to and sang with contemporary worship songs, but also with adaptations of theologically brilliant old hymns. If you have a skewed vision of God, reading the lyrics of traditional hymns and singing them will help you understand the nature of God.

Bible Study

Another thing I did when I became a Christian was to buy a concordance (a reference book listing every Bible verse under a key word from that verse) and a basic one-volume biblical commentary to accompany the Bible my coworker Jeff got me.

Knowing the nature of God through His Word is a powerful weapon we can use to overcome same-sex attractions. The Bible says that "the word of God is living and active and sharper than any two-edged sword, and piercing as far as the division of soul and spirit, of both joints and marrow, and able to judge the thoughts and intentions of the heart" (Hebrews 4:12 NASB).

It is through God's Word that we will learn the secret desires of our hearts and what motivates us. My friend LeNair used to spend hours after work studying her Bible. She didn't just read it; she got into it. She motivated me to do the same through a simple statement that has stuck with me over the years. With her Bible, commentaries, and concordance sprawled in front of her, LeNair said, "The more I dig into the Bible to learn about God, the more I learn about me." That is the nature of God! To give back to us above and beyond what we have given to Him of our time, thoughts, and energy.

As you study or read the Bible, write down God's promises so you can refer to them when you're going through tough times. You can also use them in your prayer times. God's promise, "the LORD your God is the one who goes with you. He will not fail you or forsake you," reminds you that you are never alone and that He will accomplish His purposes in your life (Deuteronomy 31:6 NASB).

You might also find it helpful to write down or underline the imperatives in your Bible, starting in the New Testament. Underline *everything* God says you need to do. That way you'll know what your responsibilities are. Some examples?

- "Flee youthful lusts" (2 Timothy 2:22).
- "Be holy yourselves also in all your behavior" (1 Peter 1:15).
- "Treat others the same way you want them to treat you" (Luke 6:31).

Once you know God's promises to you and your responsibilities to God, memorize those scriptures so they'll instantly come to mind when you need them.

As you continue on this life-changing journey by embracing the freedom you have in Christ, you'll experience times of tremendous joy and excitement. You'll also experience times of disheartening weariness and disappointment. Just remember what the apostle Paul wrote to the Galatians: "Let us not lose heart in doing good, for in due time we will reap if we do not grow weary" (Galatians 6:9 NASB).

> When you are completely God's, you are completely free.

Don't give up! Soon it will be your time to reap the fruits of righteousness.

Let me close by quoting Mother Teresa. When talking to a reporter, she put it simply: "It is nothing extraordinary to be holy. Holiness is not the luxury of the few. Holiness is a simple duty for you and for me. We have been created for that." In another interview, she explained the concept of surrendering completely to Jesus: "Jesus said, 'I have chosen you, I have called you by your name, you are Mine.' Every day you have to say, 'Yes.' Total surrender...You are free then."

When you are completely His, you are completely free.

8

Same-Sex Attraction and Marriage

by Mike Goeke

A Note from Alan

I've asked my friend Mike Goeke to address the aspects of leaving homosexuality from the point of view of a married man.

Married Yet Gay?

I stood across the kitchen from my wife. We stared at each other. I had just asked her to take me back after a several month separation, during which time I had fully explored life as a gay man.

We had no idea what to do. We were facing a battle that a lifetime in the church had done nothing to prepare us for. The conflict seemed incredibly daunting. Yet somehow we both knew God was calling us to fight for our marriage. And so my wife opened the door to reconciliation, and we began an incredible journey.

A Married Man's Priorities

Dealing with unwanted homosexual feelings and desires is very much the same whether we are married or single—as least as it relates to us personally. But practically speaking there are several differences.

In my experience, married men usually don't publicly identify themselves as gay. They often have strong community and familial relationships with people who are not gay. Their lives are not focused around the gay community or the gay subculture. Most of the time their sexual experiences are centered on pornography, online hook-ups, or anonymous encounters. If they've had a "relationship" with another man, it was likely very secretive.

Married men also have different realities that may help motivate them to pursue change. They obviously have wives with whom, despite any struggles in their marriage, they have formed spiritual unions through the bond of marriage. They often have children whose lives will be hugely impacted by the choices their dads make. And a married man faces leaving the familiar world he knows if he chooses to enter the gay-identified world.

But perhaps the most important difference is that a married man has dedicated his life to another person and made a vow before God affirming this commitment. Thus, his life is not his own. His role as a husband should take precedence over his sexual attractions. A family man is best able to realize that his journey is not just about himself.

To the world outside the Christian church, culture has painted homosexuality as a condition set in stone. It scoffs at the idea that a marriage between a man and a woman can survive when one spouse battles same-sex attractions. Yet even in the midst of situations that seem impossible, many couples know deep in their hearts that divorce is not the answer. Husbands who battle intense same-sex desires want desperately to be free. They want to be the husbands God has called them to be.

Many wives in this situation choose to see past their husbands' indiscretions and struggles to see men full of potential, men God has placed with them, men present for a divine purpose. These are not couples content to live a twisted, dual life of sexual freedom and extramarital sexual liaisons. These are marriages where the partners are trusting that God will forgive them, grow them, restore them, and honor their commitment to their marital vows. These are marriages that are not just surviving, but are thriving in the way that can only happen through the power of God's intense work in your life.

Keep in mind that no two marriages are exactly alike. So as you read this chapter, take what fits your marriage and apply it. Ask God to give you hope and help as you fight for your marriage. He hates divorce. He loves to change lives. He designed your marriage to bring Him glory. *He will fight for that with you.*

Why Are You Here?

As with anyone leaving homosexuality, your motives and your expectations are very important and should be assessed. Often married men will stay in their marriages for the kids, because they don't want to be alone, because they don't want people to know about their struggles, because divorce is a sin, or for many other reasons. While these reasons aren't invalid or wrong per se, if any of these is the singular or even primary reason for staying in your marriage, your chances of success, transformation, and restoration are weakened.

As Alan has pointed out, heterosexuality isn't your primary goal, and neither should your goal be limited to the legal survival of your marriage. God is not honored by two people married on paper and living separate and/or miserable lives. God will transform your marriage! But you must be open to His transforming power. Are you committed first to following God and to fully setting yourself apart as a follower of Christ? Are you committed to your marriage

> Your struggles may get more intense before they get better, but your commitment to God and to your marriage will help you and your spouse endure the refining work of God.

and to allowing God to change you as an individual while He rebuilds your marriage into one that honors Him and brings Him glory?

Before you decide to undertake this journey, assess your heart. What you decide to do should depend on nothing but what *God* is telling you to do. Seek Him and His wisdom. Then express your commitment to your spouse…and express it often. Your struggles may get more intense before they get better, but your commitment to God and to your marriage will help you and your spouse endure the refining work of God. He will forge a new marriage that will bring you joy and Him glory.

Accepting Your New Reality

If you're reading this book, you have likely been thrust into a reality you wish was just a bad dream. That was certainly my experience. I recall lying in bed and wanting desperately to go back in time to have a "do over." But reality is reality, and simply "going to a happy place" won't help for very long. Coming to grips and understanding your reality are important steps toward your healing and the restoration of your marriage. Can you relate to one of these situations?

- Your wife discovered evidence on the computer that you've been engaging in viewing homosexual pornography or other activity geared toward men.

- Your wife received a phone call or intercepted a message or was otherwise informed that you were engaging in some form of extramarital behavior with another man.

- Your wife sensed something was going on and, acting on a whim, asked you if anything was wrong. You admitted you were struggling with homosexual feelings or engaging is some sort of homosexual behavior.

- A medical test came back indicating a positive HIV result or some other STD, which exposed your extramarital behavior.

- Burdened with guilt and shame, you confessed your homosexual struggle to your spouse and expressed your desire to get help and save the marriage.

- You admitted to your wife that although you haven't acted out with another man in any way, you've been burdened intensely by same-sex attractions.

Your wife may be angry and hurt. As a result she may have shut you out of her life. She is likely very afraid. She may even be living in denial. Or perhaps her response was to tell you to get all this homosexuality stuff fixed and let her know when you're done. She may want to talk about it constantly or may never want to talk about it at all.

All the while, your desires may be fierce. You may be grieving the loss of a same-sex relationship or the reality that you will never again be able to act out in ways that brought you such pleasure. You may be angry and scared. You may be ashamed and humiliated. Whatever your feelings and situation, you must accept them as your reality in order to move past them.

Even if none of those scenarios fits you exactly or if your situation is a combination of them, the end result is usually very similar. The worst thing you can do is pretend nothing is wrong. While it may seem hopeless to you, this is an opportunity for you and your wife to grow as individuals and for your marriage to grow into a relationship far beyond what you could possibly imagine.

Out in the Open

With your homosexual struggle out in the open, there will most likely be some dramatic emotions surfacing. Remember, emotions are neither good nor bad. In fact, emotions are *always* gifts from God (even the very difficult ones) and are designed by Him to draw you to Him. The only bad thing to do with emotions is to deny them. The truth is that God desires you to take all your emotions to Him and to shine the light of His Word and His love on them. When your emotions compel you to Him, they achieve their perfect result.

Men who have hidden a secret struggle with homosexuality for many years are often adept at shutting down and numbing their emotions. If this is you, you may now experience heavy and unfamiliar emotions. You may find yourself unsure how to feel without running to some source to numb the powerful feelings. Your marriage has been rocked, but even more, your deep, personal struggle has also been revealed. You can expect to feel some or all of these emotions.

- *Anger.* You may feel angry at being exposed, angry at yourself for falling prey to sin, angry at your spouse for her lack of understanding, and angry at God for allowing you to struggle with something as intense as these homosexual desires.

You may also feel a general sense of anger with no specific object.

- *Fear.* Fear of the unknown can cripple you. Fear of being alone, fear of disease, fear related to finances, fear of more exposure, and fear of losing your children are just a few of the likely problems you'll experience.

- *Grief.* While your behavior may have been wrong or sinful, it likely was fueled by the mistaken fantasy that you could have both worlds. The exposure of your struggle and your submission to help and healing will often bring a sense of grief. You may grieve the loss of the fantasy, the loss of activity that met a perceived need in you (even though in a wrong way), the loss of your dreams and hopes, and the loss of innocence and/or trust in your marriage.

- *Sadness, depression, sorrow.* Extreme sadness and brokenheartedness are common in these situations for obvious reasons. You may find yourself constantly on the verge of tears, crying uncontrollably, or crying at seemingly random or inopportune times.

- *Hopelessness.* The road ahead may seem too hard. Your fears may seem so real and powerful they're insurmountable.

- *Frustration.* The lack of control over the situation or over your spouse's attitudes or responses to you may cause you great frustration.

- *Vulnerability, insecurity.* Your place as the wrongdoer in the marriage may cause you to feel vulnerable. You may feel very insecure about your future and all that is before you.

- *Shame, embarrassment.* The deep and often long-time struggle with homosexuality usually brings shame from an early age. The exposure of that struggle increases shame and embarrassment.

- *Relief.* It's not uncommon to feel great relief that your secret is finally being released, even in the midst of all the other emotions.

- *Hope.* Getting everything out in the open and being honest with each other may give you hope for the future.

- *Lack of faith.* Hard realities in our lives often cause us to question God and rocks our faith in Him.

- *Desperation.* You may feel desperate for help. You want someone or something to fix your situation. You may also experience a desperation or dependency on God like you've never experienced before.

- *Loneliness, isolation.* Whether others know your issue or not, you will likely feel very alone as you process all you're going through.

- *Guilt.* You will likely experience great guilt as you realize the full extent of hurt caused by your actions.

- *Blame.* You may find yourself looking for someone or something to blame for how you feel and all that has happened to you.

- *Sense of entitlement.* You may find yourself dwelling on what you feel you deserve or don't deserve.

- *Brokenness.* As you begin the process of dealing with your same-sex leanings, you will likely see and understand your sin and your need for a Savior in a new and profound way.

- *Graciousness and mercy.* You may find yourself surprisingly gracious and merciful toward your spouse. Your recognition of God's (and hopefully your spouse's) grace toward you will likely give you a great and sweet grace for others.

- *Misunderstood.* The array of myths and misunderstandings (especially in the church) about homosexuality may cause you to feel hopelessly misunderstood and condemned.

Your spouse is likely dealing with many new emotions too. She is likely feeling some or all of these emotions.

- *Anger* at you, at God, or a general anger directed at innocent parties.

- *Fear* of being alone, fear of disease, fear related to finances, and fear for your children.

- *Grief* at losing part of herself or her hopes and dreams for her life.

- *Sadness, depression, and sorrow* for obvious reasons. She may be constantly on the verge of tears, crying uncontrollably, or crying at seemingly random or inopportune times.

- *Hopelessness* because the road ahead may seem too hard or the fears may seem so real and insurmountable.

- *Vulnerability and insecurity* over the broken trust in your marriage may cause her to feel very exposed to more hurt. She may feel very insecure about the future and all that is before her.

- *Shame and embarrassment* at the infidelity in marriage on top of the shame or embarrassment that the struggle is homosexual.

- *Relief* that she finally discovered the truth.

- *Hope* that getting everything out in the open and being honest with each other may heal the situation.

- *Lack of faith* due to the hard realities. She may question God and her faith in Him.

- *Desperate* for help or for someone or something to fix the situation. She may also experience a desperation or dependency on God like she's never experienced before.

- *Loneliness and isolation* because of the nature of the situation.

- *Guilt* as she wonders what she did or didn't do to cause or contribute to this situation.
- *Blame* as she looks for someone or something as a cause for all that is happening to her.
- *Sense of entitlement* as she dwells on what she feels she deserves or doesn't deserve.
- *Vengeance* because she wants to get you back for what you have done to her.
- *Brokenness* as the exposure of your struggle causes her to see and understand her own sin and her own need for a Savior in a new and profound way.
- *Graciousness and mercy* toward you, although she may be surprised and wonder if such feelings are okay.
- *Betrayal* by you, someone in whom she had great and deep trust.

As you deal with your own emotions, remember your spouse is handling her emotions too. You may be experiencing some of the same emotions but for different reasons. As you go to God with your struggles, pray for your spouse. Beginning this process of leaving homosexuality mindful of what your spouse is struggling with is an important part of restoring your relationship and growing into the husband God desires you to be.

Your emotions may change day-to-day. Some of them may not manifest themselves until days, months, or years down the road. Some may cycle, based on other issues in your lives. You may not "conquer" these emotions, and they may return.

Remember, emotions arise for a purpose—to drive you to God for truth, grace, growth, and maturity.

No, there is no checklist that will help signify an end to this process. But don't expect to be sad forever either. God will sustain you, strengthen you, reveal Himself to you, and grow joy in you at each step! This journey is well worth the effort.

The Disclosure

One of the most difficult parts of rebuilding your marriage is dealing with the disclosure. Nothing is harder than admitting your indiscretions and failures to your wife. Because homosexuality often brings with it feelings of shame and self-hatred, it's especially hard to share. But disclosure is an important part of the healing. It opens the door for an amazing openness and honesty in your relationship. While sharing struggles and failures with my wife has been hard, it has also helped us build a life together that is based on honesty and vulnerability. We wouldn't trade this part of our marriage for anything now.

You have likely disclosed something at this point, and more than likely you would be content to leave it at that. Your wife may not be quite that way. She may want to know more. The questions and images in her mind could be very intense and controlling. You will both need to make some concessions in the area of disclosure. You may need to tell more than you really want to tell, and she may need to accept that there are details she doesn't need to know.

> Telling no one is not the answer. Both of you need godly people involved for support, help, and accountability.

You and your wife need to seek godly counsel in dealing with disclosure issues. It's best to *plan* disclosure, include an unbiased third party, and be in a neutral and safe location. The location where full disclosure takes place will likely be forever associated with that meeting, so it's important that it not be your living room, your favorite restaurant, or any place you frequent.

Views on what to disclose differ. At the least you should be ready to share the general nature of your extramarital activities, such as whether the activity involved other people or was limited to pornography or fantasy. Be prepared to share where the activities generally occurred. Your wife has a right to know how many other people were involved and the general time frame of your activities. Your spouse may have a right to know the names of your partners, especially if they are people she knows.

My wife and I agree that it is not best for a wife to know specific details of sexual experiences or sexual acts. We also believe that information disclosed should, for the most part, be kept confidential between the spouses. Absent extreme circumstances, it is not your place or your wife's place to reveal someone else's struggle.

Questions often arise regarding whether or not to tell friends or family what is going on in your lives and marriage. Your wife may not want anyone to know, and you may be desperate for some form of support. Or your wife may want to let others in, and you may be adamant that no one else know what is going on. To be honest, at first spouses rarely agree on who should know their struggles. These are difficult decisions to make.

Generally, telling no one is not the answer. Both of you need godly people involved for support, help, and accountability. Who to tell and how many people to tell ultimately is a decision made between both of you. If there is any desire to tell out of spite, or anger, or vengeance, or if there is a desire not to tell out of pride or fear, then your reasoning is probably unsound. Telling a friend of the struggle in your marriage doesn't mean you tell the friend every detail of what your spouse said or did or how he or she reacted. Respect the privacy of your spouse. Pray for direction, pray that your hearts will be pure in the process, and pray specifically for those with whom you will share what's happening.

Unfortunately, everyone does not respond positively to the sort of information you will be sharing. Be prepared for disappointing outcomes. Be careful too of people who give worldly or secular counsel. Disclosure should be limited to people who have evidenced a Christian worldview and a commitment to doing the right thing, no matter the cost. Even in the church, you may find people who encourage divorce or encourage accepting a gay identity.

Disclosing to children is also a frequent and difficult issue. Whether to tell your children is a question that needs to be immersed in prayer. Small children usually have no reason to know details. Older children may need to know for various reasons. It's okay to share that you are struggling without giving details. Children of any age may sense problems or issues between you and your wife. Being honest with them is important, but even more important is letting them know that you love them and that you are working to save your family. Never use the kids against your spouse or get them involved as go-betweens.

Issues of disclosure are painful and usually surface early in the process. Don't take this lightly. Seek the Lord. Seek godly counsel from your pastor or counselor. While this issue is hard, it's an opportunity to begin a new life of honesty and openness between you and your wife. Few couples have the level of emotional intimacy you will likely grow in your marriage, and that is a blessing (born out of struggle).

Forgiveness and Rebuilding Trust

In almost every situation where homosexuality invades a marriage, there are actions that require forgiveness. In most cases, the trust between you and your wife has been shattered due to your behavior. You have very likely hurt your wife and destroyed her trust in you. Reestablishing trust is primarily *your* responsibility.

Search your heart and determine if you are truly sorry. If you aren't, then you and God need to deal with that before you proceed. Most men I have worked with are truly sorry. They hate what they've done and wish desperately that they could turn back the clock. But they also know that things are so messed up inside them—things that their wives probably won't fully understand. These things might also give a "why" for your acting out behaviors.

Unfortunately, forgiveness and rebuilding trust require the participation of both parties to work best. You cannot control your wife; you can only control you. Hopefully, your wife is getting wise counsel too. Even if she isn't, you can do the right thing. You must ask forgiveness, and you must repent. You need to ask forgiveness without conditions or detailed explanations. A very simple "I am sorry for…" is all you can really say. Your heart must be turning away from the behavior. Changing behavior is very hard. Hang in there!

Asking for forgiveness is actually the easier part. Forgiveness generally happens at a specific time and place and is an act of will in many ways. Rebuilding trust takes time...and often lots of it. Your role in the process is simple—you must *earn* the trust back. Should she choose to accept it, your wife's role in the process is to allow the trust to be rebuilt.

To earn back trust, you must do whatever it takes to show your wife that you want her to trust you again. Let her set the rules. What might this look like? You may need to...

- check in by phone
- account for every minute of every day for a while
- not do things with your friends or people from work
- disconnect the Internet at home
- turn down work requests to travel
- change jobs
- quit the gym

Are you willing to do whatever it takes? Is rebuilding trust that important to you? I hope so.

Hopefully, trust rebuilding will only take a season. In my case, after a couple of years we realized that trust had been restored. I had willingly curtailed my freedoms, and my wife graciously, over time, allowed me to regain those freedoms. She never treated me like a child or like a felon, because, according to her, she could see how much I wanted her to trust me again. Make sure you're willing, and make sure your wife can see how willing you are. Do your part to make this process work. Trust that God will honor your commitments.

Sex

It's not uncommon for couples impacted by homosexuality to have sexual issues. Wives who discover their husbands struggle with same-sex attraction will react in different ways. Some may decide they don't want any physical intimacy with their husbands. Trust has been broken, they have unwanted images in their minds, and they just won't make themselves that vulnerable. Other wives may want to have sex all the time. They may equate sex as a sign that you're attracted to them. Or maybe they get validation of their desirability through sexual activity.

In many cases, the husband may struggle with sexual performance. Sometimes the reality is that his body doesn't respond easily to the female body. Sometimes the problem is pressure, anxiety, or depression. The memories of past sexual acts with other men or pornographic images may so fill his mind that he can't perform sexually with his wife. In most cases I've seen, even when these things are true, the husband desperately wants to have a good, healthy sex life with his spouse.

Sex between a husband and wife is a vital part of the marital relationship. God designed the marital relationship to be one of relational *and* physical intimacy. Even if it seems that you can do without sex, at some point it will become an issue that needs to be addressed.

When my wife and I started on our journey to healing and health, we took a mutually agreed upon break from sex. My wife didn't really want to connect with me physically due to the lack of trust. And I felt so much pressure sexually that I would become an emotional mess. A few months into our process, I realized it was time to work through the sex issue. We began to see my counselor as a couple specifically to work through rebuilding our physical relationship. He creatively helped us work through many years of sexual dysfunction.

I've learned that every marriage faces struggles in the bedroom. We weren't alone. Many heterosexual men have shared sexual issues in their marriages with me. Often the answer is simply to talk about sex together. I've shared with my wife my feelings, my desires, my triggers, and that sex with her is not as much about lust as it is about relationship. She has accepted that I am different and realizes that my sexual feelings and struggles do not diminish my love and commitment to her.

She also has her own sexual issues and struggles. As we share openly with each other, our relationship and sex life grows stronger.

I now realize that sex with my wife is pure. In that purity, and in the context of our marital and spiritual bond, it is much, much more satisfying than sex with a man (no matter how lust-filled that sex was). The thrill of satisfying my wife, the sense of peace in lying quietly with her afterward and drifting to sleep, and the miraculous way our sexual bond builds true and lasting intimacy exceed the sexual experiences to which I thought I was entitled. In the early days of my process I was anxious that I would never have good sex again. I need not have worried. I traded cheap, flashy sex for priceless physical intimacy with my wife.

Getting Help

You will need help to deal with your same-sex attraction issues. You can't just disclose and expect to move on. The help you need may differ from the help someone else needs. You may need to find an ex-gay support group. You'll want to pray through whether that's a healthy place for you. You may need to find a counselor. Pray through that choice too. There might not be anything available in your area in the form of counseling or support groups for your issues. If so, you may have to be more diligent to find help. I found nothing locally when my wife and I reconciled. I relied heavily on a counselor who knew little about homosexuality but a lot about Jesus. That counsel, plus books, long-distance support from people I met through Exodus International conferences, and my church helped immensely.

I encourage you to read everything you can on the subject of homosexuality and leaving homosexuality. I also encourage you to develop a friendship with someone who has never dealt with homosexuality. Make sure you can share your struggle with him. Don't tell everyone, but do find someone to tell. And don't expect that person to latch on to you, be your savior, and lead you out of your issues. That's not his job!

You will also need to find someone to hold you accountable. Again, this person is ideally someone who does not share your struggle. Your wife shouldn't be your primary accountability partner either. Find a man you trust and isn't a trigger, someone who can handle the ins and outs of what pushes your buttons. Be honest and share what you need.

Finally, be careful to not overcommit to your personal recovery. You don't want your marriage to fall by the wayside. I've seen men who run to support groups every chance they get while their wives sit at home alone. There are not many resources for spouses, so tend to your marriage. As a married man, you are no longer your own. Spend time cultivating and healing your marriage. In that process, you may see more healing happen in you personally than you imagined possible.

Conclusion

As I wrestled with God about whether I could really "go home" and live a happy life as a married man, He constantly repeated to my soul three simple words: "I love you." In those words, I saw a powerful Savior who would never call me to do something and then send me out alone.

My counselor encouraged me to write down God's promises as I read them in the Bible, and one of those promises really sustained me in the early days. John 10:10 says that Jesus came so that we might have life—and have it in abundance. Life didn't seem very abundant at the time, but *I chose to believe* that promise. When I became depressed, I repeated it over and over in my head. Eventually I began to *feel* it. And now, many years down the road, I can see that God fulfilled that promise...and continues to fulfill that promise in my life. He has set up perfect boundaries and guidelines for each of us who follows Him

God can do above and beyond anything we can ask or imagine. Submit your imagination to Him. Even if you can't see how everything will work out, trust that He will work beyond the ability of your human mind to craft something beautiful. The ride may be bumpy at times, but it's *so* worth it. Claim God's promise of abundance and wait expectantly as He unfolds it in your life.

Part 4

Staying the
Course

9

Dealing with Temptations and Critics

You have made a decision to follow Christ. And that's great! Unfortunately, you'll face some opposition. Certainly temptations will oppose your walk with God. And so will critics.

Change isn't the absence of struggle. Rather it's having freedom amid that struggle to choose a better course. Engrave that in your mind. Temptation will happen today, tomorrow, and 20 years from now. Don't be shocked when it presents itself even when you think life is going smoothly.

I gave up homosexuality a long time ago, but I'm not deluded enough to think I don't have to be careful. When I'm driving home from hanging out with my buddies, when I travel, and when I'm on the Internet I make good use of accountability filters. I am human, and humans are prone to fail. Temptation could come at any time. It is God in me that makes me the success I am today as I daily choose to surrender my wants, desires, and bents to His Lordship.

There are other things that help me as well. I call them road blocks, and I've been establishing them behind me every step of the way for 18 years now. We've already talked about a lot of them: accountability, healthy same-sex friendships, my love for my wife and kids, and most importantly my love for the Lord.

Another strong deterrent is calling to mind some of the uglier moments from the old days. We all have those haunting and awful memories. They can serve as sober reminders that what we have today is far better than what we used to settle for. For example, I will never forget the last night I had sex with a man. I came home to my apartment furious that I had given in again. I couldn't believe I'd forgotten how much I hated the moments immediately following climax—the most sober moments a sex addict ever has. The flood of reality that pours in, painfully reminding me that what I spent hours hunting for and anticipating as this amazing thrill…is really a measly little wizard behind the curtain. It may have an all-powerful voice, but once obeyed it fails to measure up—and miserably so. I know you know that. We all do.

> Truly, no same-sex encounter is worth the riches you'll be given in Christ Jesus.

That night I came in around three in the morning and couldn't get to my shower fast enough. I scrubbed my body and wept as if I had been mortally wounded. Then and there I made a vow to God that I have kept to this day…15 years now. *I will never give myself to any man and, beyond that, to anyone other than a wife—if God sees fit to give me one.*

I remember every detail of that shower, that wailing, and that prayer. I asked God to never erase it from my memory for this very purpose: to remind me, should temptation arise, that *what my flesh craves has no ability to satisfy.* On the contrary, it will destroy me.

I also have been given the great ability—a permanent buzz kill, if you will—to imagine every temptation through to completion before I give in to it. If I'm tempted to fantasize or masturbate, I see that fantasy through to labeling it as committing adultery against my Lord, my wife, and my kids. I picture appearing before the Lord broken over what I've done. I can see myself getting into bed with my wife after falling and knowing I can never regain what was lost. I don't want that. I hate that. No temptation or moment of sexual pleasure is worth the cost of sinning against Jesus or destroying this present life that I cherish and love.

If you aren't married or don't have kids, I pray that your relationship with the Lord grows to the point that you come to love Him and the life He has given you more than the pleasure that comes in a moment of climax. Truly, no same-sex encounter is worth the riches you'll be given in Christ Jesus.

As you grow in the Christian life, you'll become more acutely aware of the trade-offs involved in going back. You'll see more clearly that it's just not worth it. When you've been invited to eat at a lush banquet table, you'd be foolish to chuck it all and go back to eating out of Dumpsters.

When all is said and done, *you* must decide that a life of giving in to sin is not who you were destined to be and that there is more for you *with Jesus*.

Identity and Renewing the Mind

So much of being gay is taking on the identity and becoming first and foremost gay. Whatever else you are, you are first, last, and always gay. Whether a male homosexual or a lesbian, there is a push to identify yourself as gay. Life becomes ordered around that. There are gay newspapers, gay magazines, gay television channels, gay tourist attractions, gay jargon, gay churches, and so on. If a man or woman is dealing with same-sex attractions, it's far easier today than it was a generation or two ago to jump into a gay-identified subculture with both feet.

For that reason, a large part of "staying the course" after leaving homosexuality is becoming rooted in your new identity in Christ. As we focus more on our lives in Him, our former identity fades slowly away.

How can we become more firmly planted in our identity in Christ? As already suggested, forgiving, being honest, accepting ourselves in our God-given gender, and finding authentic community help. Another important aspect is to change the way we think. The Bible calls this "renewing our minds." Here is a key verse that encourages us in this important step:

> Do not conform any longer to the pattern of this world, but
> be transformed by the renewing of your mind. Then you will

be able to test and approve what God's will is—his good, pleasing and perfect will (Romans 12:2).

Interestingly and importantly, the verse preceding this also tells us how to think about our bodies:

I urge you, brothers, in view of God's mercy, to offer your bodies as living sacrifices, holy and pleasing to God—this is your spiritual act of worship (Romans 12:1).

People who do not accept Jesus may do what they wish with their bodies. But not Christians. In a very real way, we no longer belong to ourselves. Our minds and our bodies belong to God:

Do you not know that your body is a temple of the Holy Spirit, who is in you, whom you have received from God? You are not your own; you were bought at a price. Therefore honor God with your body (1 Corinthians 6:19-20).

When we grasp that truth and apply it by faith to our daily lives, we become stronger in our identities as God's children and His dear possessions.

Study the Bible regularly and passionately. It shows His love for us. It instructs us in daily living. As we read and meditate on God's Word, our minds are renewed...*washed*, really. Read the Bible as God's special message just for you and let it penetrate and refresh you daily.

God's ultimate goal for you, as revealed in Romans 8:29 NASB, is that you be "conformed to the image of His Son." Wow! What a destiny! That will happen as you yield your mind and body to Him.

Plateaus

At some point in your journey, you may reach a plateau. You'll feel stuck. You're not going forward but not really going backward either. You're stalled.

That happened to me. I'd been a leader in post-gay ministry, a worship leader at my church, and found a measure of success in my personal life. Yet I found myself losing sight of the blessings in store for me if I stayed focused on the Lord. Prior to meeting Leslie, I settled into an unhealthy emotional friendship with a fellow struggler, thinking that was the best human relationship I was going to get. I was making short-term decisions that were beginning to affect my long-term goals. I was not in a good place, and it was because I'd spent so much of my journey focused on what I was leaving behind, on what I was giving up, that I lost focus on what was ahead.

> Discovering our identity in Christ is a joyful and life-long process.

That year was pivotal for me. Thankfully, the unhealthy friendship suffered a rift and I was forced to look elsewhere for people to spend time with. As I found friends that weren't tied to the issues I was battling, I began filling my social time with a variety of godly people...and with God. This finally helped me get to the next level of growth in my relationship with Christ. I also learned the important lesson of not looking for my hope and security in another person. Christ alone is my base!

Overcoming insecurity by finding your security in Christ is a huge milestone. Those of us who struggle with homosexuality are among the most insecure people on the planet. Ideally, our insecurities will drive us to Christ and cause us to remember our firm position *in Him.* The great secret of victory is to never see ourselves outside of Christ. Colossians 2:10 tells us we are complete in Christ. When we fully grasp that in Christ we are whole men and women, our insecurities (and many temptations) will fade away.

So much of our growth as Christians—no matter what our issues— is discovering our new and complete identity in Christ. It's a joyful and lifelong process as more and more of our riches in Christ are made real to us.

You What?

Your decision to pursue a life beyond homosexuality by putting your faith before your sexual attractions is going to be hard for some of your family members and friends to understand. If you've spent any amount of time "out of the closet" and gathered a group of people that support gay life around you, this change will probably evoke a strong reaction. They might respond very cautiously at best or harshly, at worst.

There are a variety of reasons for negative reactions from family and friends. One reason is they love you. Depending on the relationship, your allies might have watched you struggle through the painful decision to accept your gay identity. And the thought of you going through another painful experience of essentially rejecting that identity causes them to want to protect you. However, if they could look ahead to the ultimate joy you're embracing, their objections would cease.

Those most likely to be angered by your decision to leave homosexuality are your gay friends. Such a decision is often seen as defecting from the homeland and turning away from those who are "your" people. A great many of your gay friends will not understand or support your decision.

When I committed to the process of leaving homosexuality, I periodically ran into gay friends in public. One friend asked me every time he saw me how my "straight-wanna-be club" was working for me. At the time his question hurt and I felt very unaccepted by him. But now I understand *he* was reacting out of his hurt. I was his friend, and he had trusted me. My decision to live a different life made him feel like I was rejecting my own homosexual struggle *and* his chosen identity *and* ultimately him. No matter how we feel about homosexuality or biblical truth, we must carefully consider how to communicate our decisions to those who might be inadvertently hurt by them.

> The strength of your decision for Christ may be tested early on by those who will ridicule or argue against your new life. Be prepared.

We also need to protect ourselves. Just as I wouldn't recommend "coming out" to everyone all at once, I don't recommend sharing the decision to leave homosexuality via an email blast to everyone. Leaving gay life is a huge decision, and you will need solid support. At this early point in your journey, you don't need a lot of people telling you you're making a mistake or giving you their version of how you ought to live your life.

For those who do react negatively, be prepared ahead of time. Let your support system know when you're going to share your decision with someone who might react badly. Ask for prayer *before* you talk. If this person lives with you, make sure you have a place to go if the discussion goes horribly wrong. And don't take any response personally. Give people time to react and then time to consider.

The strength of your decision for Christ may be tested early on by those who will ridicule or argue against your new life. Be prepared.

10

This Is the Life We Were Created to Live

For those of us who take this walk out of homosexuality, we see our same-sex attractions as the vehicle—the need in our lives—that brought us to faith in Christ. We need to go on from there and embrace a destiny that's far beyond merely dealing with our sexual issues.

Through my work at Exodus, I've come to see that this ministry has given me the opportunity to talk about the real mission we all have: helping people see and become all that God created them to be.

The media calls Exodus International all the time, asking us about our "programs" for gay people and how we "cure" people. The gay activist community is constantly trying to expose us as people who give gay-identified people false hope that homosexuality is something that can be left behind. But as you've read in this book, you've seen there is no 12-step program that will change you from gay to straight. There are no cures or formulas for eliminating same-sex attraction. What there is, however, is God's strength and support as you dedicate yourself to a successful Christian walk of holiness, which brings freedom.

Acknowledge the false promise of the homosexual life and continue to build on the foundation God has laid for you.

When I did this, I didn't forget where I came from. And I realize I won't ever come to the place in my life where I can live as though I'd never experienced same-sex attractions. I look at it this way: Some people who grow up dirt poor think success means becoming exceedingly rich. When they attain their riches, they pretend they didn't come from where they did. Or they become so entrenched in their new lives that they despise anyone who is dirt poor. In truth, none of us can live honestly as though we came from anywhere other than where we did. So why try?

I battled same-sex attractions for years. To this day I must stay focused on everything the Lord has for me to stay strong and free. That's reality…my reality. The same will likely be true for you. The real meaning of why we're here on earth is far greater than any issues we struggle with.

If you've responded positively to this book and asked Christ into your life without reservation, you are beginning! You will necessarily focus on your current trials in order to understand them, address them, and move beyond them. But don't keep your focus on only your struggles for long periods of time. I'm not saying you can deal with your stuff and then convince yourself you won't ever struggle again. What I *am* saying is that those struggles and your recovery from them are not your number one mission and focus. Pleasing God is your primary goal. Acknowledge your problems, seek help, employ what you learn, choose to live a life of godliness, and go out and live for God.

> Change takes time. How long? That's up to you and God.

Change takes time. How long? That's up to you and God. Allow the time necessary, but don't get bogged down.

When I was leading Exchange, a local Exodus Member Ministry, I knew people who wanted to stay in support groups and counseling for years. Support groups are great for a season, but they are stepping-stones—not a place to live. At the beginning of my journey, Exchange was a temporary place for me to learn, kind of like going to school. But we don't attend school forever. Eventually we learn the necessary tools for living and move on. After leaving homosexuality and when you're strong enough, you're going to be on your own. You won't need a retirement school for perpetual care.

Will you be healed? I wasn't. Not entirely, anyway. But I had gained all the knowledge from that one resource I was going to gain. I learned enough to be responsible and mature enough to be in charge of my own healing. No one at Exchange or Exodus or in counseling can tell me anything about my homosexual struggle and recovery that I don't already know. If I needed help today I wouldn't go back to Exchange. I would seek help from my pastor, my accountability friends, and my wife. I don't need to go back to elementary school to get a refresher on the basics. I need to employ what I've learned in the mature ways those basics taught me.

I encourage you to not let your mission get hijacked. God wants you to have freedom so you can enjoy life, yes, but He wants it even more because He created you for a purpose.

What Do You Have to Offer?

So many of us affected by unwanted homosexuality grow up feeling "less than." We sometimes feel like damaged goods compared to our counterparts that haven't struggled as we have. I grew up feeling like less of a boy, which later led to me feeling less of a man, and ultimately less of a Christian because of this struggle. The truth is that we are *not* less, no matter what we are tempted by or have given in to. "All have sinned and fall short of the glory of God" (Romans 3:23 NASB). Your particular sin issue isn't bigger, worse, more egregious, or harder to heal than anyone else's. And don't let anyone convince you otherwise.

As you enter into a church fellowship or as you begin to experience healing as a member of a Christian church, tell yourself the truth. Focus most on who and what God says you are. Don't allow the attitudes of the enemy (inside or outside the church) rob you of your identity.

You are the righteousness of God in Christ Jesus.

You are a child of God.

You have been given all you need to live a happy and prosperous life.

That's what you share with all the "formers" in the body of Christ. Every person you sit next to at church is some kind of "former"...or will someday be a "former."

When someone is going on and on about how awful homosexual sin is, remember that if the truth were told about his or her sins, that person wouldn't be so bold about pointing fingers at others. Christ never points at us to tell us how bad we are and then abandons us. He opens His arms to us and shows us how He created us to be. He beckons us to follow Him into the amazing lives He designed for us. Christ died for all of us. We are *all* sinners in need of saving.

Your Destiny

My good friend Dennis Jernigan is a singer and songwriter. Actually, he is more than just that—he is a psalmist. He came out of homosexuality many years ago, has since married and is the father of nine children. His music was born out of a heart of gratefulness, healing, and destiny. A few years back he wrote these words. He's given me permission to share it with you. I hope this song will help you declare yourself and be a catalyst to see and move into all that God created you to be.

This Is My Destiny

All I was I lay aside now dead to my sin, to God alive.
Born again into a new identity.
Once asleep to God in sin now wakened by the blood and cleansed.
Born again to be who He called me to be.
All I have I lay aside—run the race to gain the prize
For the sake of knowing Jesus Christ in me.
I cannot yet fully see all I'm truly called to be
Knowing Christ reveals my hope and destiny.

He calls me Child. He calls me to His side eternally.
He calls what once was lost now found; once bound to sin—now free.
He calls me holy. Calls me righteous. By the blood redeemed.
He calls me overcomer crowned with victory.
This is my destiny.

What once bound me is no more. What was stolen is restored
By the resurrection power of my King.
What was old has been made new; lies and doubts replaced by truth.
What was silent now resounds, "I am redeemed!"

He calls me servant; calls me warrior; calls me royalty.
He calls me resurrected one. He calls me His redeemed.
He calls me higher; calls me far beyond my wildest dream.
He calls my heart to come and be all He can see.
This is my destiny!

He calls me chosen. *New* creation. Trophy of His grace.
He gives me strength to fight the fight and run to win the race.
He tells me He delights in me while singing over me,
Accepting me as His beloved bride-to-be.
This is my destiny. This is my destiny.

Your Calling

We weren't designed to sit on the sidelines of life. And contrary to what some people want to pigeonhole us into, we weren't designed to *only* minister to "our own kind." Christians who believe that no one can or should minister to gay-identified people except someone who used to be involved in homosexual life are wrong. I needed Kirk and my friend Tom and all the men who helped me who hadn't struggled with homosexuality.

Develop a resolve to do all God has called you to accomplish. Work on the ability to know when to stay and when to move on. Put on a tough exterior…while keeping your heart pliable. I've gotten where I am today—in every circumstance—by praying for direction, seeking counsel, and listening to God's voice.

I was never asked to do anything I'm doing. I wouldn't have my job if I'd listened to the advice of people. I wouldn't be happily married if I had taken off after Leslie told me we had no future as a couple. We wouldn't have kids if we'd believed infertility was the end of the line for us. I wouldn't have anything if I let fear of failure or rejection harness me. And if I had listened to the lies of the enemy spoken through people—sometimes well-meaning people—I would not be walking in all that God has for me. My battle cry is "I will not be limited by any person." Don't allow people to limit you or keep you from God's calling on your life.

Test everything. Pray about everything. Run what you hear through the filter of Scripture and pray some more. Get proficient at hearing the Lord's voice and understanding the prompting of the Holy Spirit. God wants your heart, your mind, and your ear. When He has it He will share with you His mission for your life.

> God loves you and
> wants to bless you!

Deal quickly with guilt. Christ has taken our sins upon Himself. *All* of them. His attitude toward us is full of mercy and grace. We are *forgiven* men and women in Christ.

I believe that as His creations, our God wants to bless us, not punish us. His first thought regarding us is how much He loves and enjoys us. When we fail to get life right, God's heart breaks for us because our failures detour us—sometimes a long way—from His best. God wants us to get it right so we can experience all He wants to give us. I imagine Him saying, "I want My people to follow Me and do what I ask so they'll be safe and I can lavish My gifts on them. I want to show them the awesome things I have planned for them."

Yes, it's true God hates sin, and our sins can keep us from receiving God's blessings. But when we're following Jesus and living for Him, God looks at us and sees our intercessor Jesus. And Jesus already took on the punishment for all our sins! Our heavenly Father does discipline us for our own good, but that's done lovingly and with our success in mind.

I don't care where you've come from on your journey—even if you haven't really started this journey or you started the moment you opened this book. If you hear nothing else from me, hear this: *God loves you and wants to bless you!* He's not sitting up in heaven waiting for you to fail so He can push the smite button. If He wanted to get rid of people for not measuring up, He would have wiped our species out long ago! Instead, God sent His Son Jesus to redeem us. "The wages of sin is death" (Romans 6:23 NASB). But for everyone who chooses to follow Jesus and believe in Him for salvation, freedom and grace are abundant. God's love is unfathomable. He loves us so much that He never loses patience with us or loses His temper. He's the best Father and God there is!

Our Purpose

Are you beginning to understand that you were created for a purpose? I know that's become somewhat of a Christian cliché because I grew up in the church hearing it. But I interpreted it as being created to follow some rules, and I learned pretty quickly what those rules were.

I learned specifically what I wasn't supposed to do much more than uncovering some great purpose for which I was created. Sure, I heard we were created to love and serve the Lord. I got that. But as I've come to know and experience the Lord more fully, I see that He has something unique in mind for me. And I know He has a unique plan in mind for you too!

When He was making me, I believe He was saying, "Alan is going to be able to do *this* and *this*. I hope he discovers all he can do because I can't wait to see him—My creation!—living life to the utmost and in the fullness of the love and joy I've created him to experience."

I believe He said that about you too as He carefully knit you together in your mother's womb (Psalm 139:13). He created you for a purpose. God made you for something amazing. Your job is to seek God and find out what that plan is.

In a few short years I'll be 40, and I don't know all of what God has in mind for me. But every morning when I wake up I ask, "What do You want me to do today, Lord? What new thing or old thing do You want me to get done? What part of Your creative intent do You want to express today?" Sometimes, He tells me clearly and sometimes He doesn't. Sometimes I listen and sometimes I don't. (Like all of us, sometimes I'm hard of hearing.)

When I think about all the people involved in the homosexual struggle (whether they perceive it as a struggle or not), I don't view them first as people who are doing something contrary to what God created them to do. Instead, I see them primarily as people God created to do something uniquely amazing who simply haven't figured it yet.

When I'm talking to a "hardened" gay activist, whether in a debate setting, a television interview, on the phone, via email, or at a protest, I look at him or her and I think, *Who did God create you to be?* I look at the work the person is doing in the gay community, and I envision what the flip side of that would be if his or her gifts were being used as God intended. I think, *She's doing this here; therefore, she's got to be good at this.* I often pray that gay activists will catch glimpses of what God created them for so they will hunger for that to become a reality.

I confess it's not always my first response to think so positively. Sometimes my first reaction is to be ticked off, to argue, to debate, to judge, and to beat myself and others up with words. Ironically, that's how I used to think God was. I pictured Him turning over tables in heaven every time I messed up.

Think the best of God. Love Him and trust Him. Look less at your failures and more at His grace. Don't be harder on yourself than God is. Sometimes I focus on the areas of my life that aren't healed. I see my shortcomings and allow my mind to run over them again and again. But God is doing a marvelous work in me, asking me to not think on those things so much. He reminds me that if there's a troublesome area of my life, He is fully able to reveal it to me and help me grow.

The Missing

I had the privilege of taking a 45-day sabbatical in 2008. I didn't have to work. I did just a tiny little bit, but I didn't have to. A lot of that time, whether I was playing with my kids, doing something as a family for Christmas, driving around visiting friends, or sitting on the couch by myself, I was really trying to tune into the Lord. And this subject of destiny and God's call that I'm talking about in this chapter was something that was really churning inside me. I started writing about it, and when I got back into the office I continued. I knew there was more to what God wanted me to say, so I kept going.

It came to me that we in the church have this description of those outside the body of Christ as "lost." Although that's an apt word for their condition, God challenged me to start referring to them as "missing" because He created each of us for a purpose. He created each and every person hoping they would choose Him and fulfill the perfect design, the unique purpose, He created them for. And when I look at the body of Christ, there's obviously some gaping holes. People are missing!

> The message of the gospel is a lot bigger than simply overcoming a problem area. It's finding real love and sharing it with others.

And oftentimes even when we are in Christ, we're not following Him to the fullest so we are missing from the body. Not lost or in jeopardy of going to hell, but missing from working together and accomplishing God's plan.

The church can always use good leaders and creative people. And the people I know who have been touched by homosexuality are some of the most innovative people God ever created. Sometimes when I look at the body of Christ and note our weaknesses, and I also look at the gay community and list their strengths, I see a mirror image. What are the strengths of the gay community? They're unified. They're sold out. They're smart. They're organized. They're creative. They're dynamic. We need these people in the body of Christ!

How about you? Have you been missing from the body of Christ or from your calling? Maybe like me you were raised in a Christian home, and much of what was written in these chapters you already know. But somewhere along the way you stepped out of your God-ordained purpose and followed your same-sex attractions. Or maybe you've never set foot in a church and all this is new to you. In either case, my prayer is not only that you leave homosexuality but that you also find a place of ministry and usefulness in the body of Christ. Use your gifts with compassion and help a hurting world.

This message of the gospel is a lot bigger than simply overcoming a problem area. It's finding real love and then sharing it with others who are dying. There are a lot of dying people in the world today. The church needs you. Enter your God-appointed destiny.

A Final Encouragement

It has long been my experience that the people freed from homosexuality and who realize their God calling become more authentic. They're more comfortable with who they are in God than many who haven't struggled with same-sex attractions. The people who overcome their distorted views of gender and sexuality could become the men and women who lead the church in discovering true, godly masculinity and femininity. God can do amazing things and promote those who were once at the bottom to the top. I know that's what He wants for you. And He'll do it for you if you give Him the opportunity.

My wife says she's thankful for my past struggles and who I am today. Who I am is exactly who she needs her husband to be. Where I once viewed my love of design, decorating, and music as "gay," she thinks are fine attributes for her man. I had allowed the enemy, through the world, to tell me I was something I wasn't simply because I wasn't stereotypically male. As I've grown and matured in Christ, He regularly tells me that I am a man He loves. He uses me—allows me—to lead men who have and haven't struggled with homosexuality. He can do the same miraculous transformation in you if you will only trust Him.

At this very moment I believe God wants to give you something. I encourage you to hold out your hands and receive it. I feel led to pray for you. Will you let me?

Amazing God, thank You for creating us. Thank You for creating each person reading this book. I love Your encouragement. I know You're saying to us now that You'd rather have a struggling, broken, desperate child than no child at all.

God, I thank You for the desperate, hurting people reading this book. Please comfort them. Whether that's through Your Word, a song, a pat on the back, a hug, a kind look, or someone who holds a door open, let them know You love them. Help them be aware of Your encouragement because it's all around them.

God, help us all see and pick up the tools You've left for us to use as we journey toward wholeness in You. Give us a glimpse of who You want us to become.

For the man who feels a lacking in his manhood and his masculinity, I ask that You encourage him where he's at. He's artistic, creative, and Your child. You created him with those gifts for a purpose. Help him use them for Your glory.

For the woman who struggles with her identity, who sees all around her women she thinks are more ideal I pray that You will break that image. Help her realize that she is who You created her to be.

Lord, I pray that You will help us see ourselves and one another as the people You created us to be. Affirm the amazing gifts You placed in us. I pray that You will help us knock down any idols we've created, the inaccurate ideals we've set up. I pray that we will look to You for our security and affirmation. Help us realize that true affirmation, love, acceptance, and healing come only in the name of Jesus Christ.

Lord, Your wealth of resources and gifts and talents that You bestow on us are overwhelming. Encourage the readers of this book with the truth. You created us for something big, and You fashioned us perfectly. We have everything we need in You to live abundant lives.

Thank You for Your Word so we can know Your goodness. Show us Your love and provision today. Show us how to reach those who are missing from the body of Christ and use us to reach them.

May we give all the praise and glory to You. In Your Son's name, I pray. Amen.

What to Do Next

1. Check out the additional resources at the end of this book.

2. Buy a good Bible. I recommend a modern version such as the updated New American Standard or the New International Version.

3. Start reading the New Testament, and then dip into the psalms.

4. Find good fellowship in a local church. Keep praying and looking until you find the right one.

5. If you need one-on-one counseling, choose a good Christian counselor. You can go to www.ExodusInternational.org or call Focus on the Family at 1-800-AFAMILY for assistance.

6. Pray often. Prayer is talking to God. Be honest with Him about your struggles and your hopes.

7. If there's anything God leads you to do as you exercise forgiveness, do it. For me, it was clearing the air with my father.

8. Attend a conference where you'll get encouragement from others who know what you're going through. When you walk through the door at an Exodus Freedom Conference and see several hundred men and women who've been where you are, you'll be overwhelmed—in a good way. Check out www.ExodusFreedom.org.

9. If you're living with a former partner, prayerfully figure out what you're going to do. Talk with a counselor. If your partner hassles you about your decision to follow Christ, you'll need to move out as soon as possible.

10. Always remember you're not just leaving something...*you're also entering something much greater.*

Recommended Resources

Books

Bickel, Bruce, and Stan Jantz. *Now That You're a Christian: A Guide to Your Faith in Plain Language.* Eugene, OR: Harvest House Publishers, 2008.

Comiskey, Andy. *The Kingdom of God and the Homosexual.* Desert Stream Press, 2007.

Dallas, Joe. *Desires in Conflict.* Eugene, OR: Harvest House Publishers, 2003.

Ensley, Mike. *Emotional Dependency for Guys.* Orlando: Exodus International.

Haley, Mike. *101 Frequently Asked Questions About Homosexuality.* Eugene, OR: Harvest House Publishers, 2004.

Hunt, June. *How to Handle Your Emotions.* Eugene, OR: Harvest House Publishers, 2008.

Konrad, Jeff. *You Don't Have to Be Gay: Hope and Freedom for Males Struggling with Homosexuality or for Those Who Know of Someone Who Is.* Newport Beach, CA: Pacific Publishing House, 1987.

Paulk, Anne. *Restoring Sexual Identity.* Eugene, OR: Harvest House Publishers, 2003.

Rentzel, Lori. *Emotional Dependency.* Orlando: Exodus International.

DVD

The Question of Homosexuality: A Conversation for Youth about Same-Sex Attraction. Eugene, OR: Harvest House Publishers, 2009.

Websites

www.AlanChambers.org (Alan's blog)

www.ExodusBooks.org

www.ExodusFreedom.org (conferences)

www.ExodusGlobalAlliance.org (ministries outside North America)

www.ExodusInternational.org

www.ExodusYouth.net

www.LoveWonOut.com

About the Authors

**Alan Chambers** is one of the nation's leading experts on gender issues and homosexuality and is the president of Exodus International—the largest Christian ministry addressing these issues in the world today. Alan's story as a young man who struggled with and overcame unwanted same-sex attraction has inspired audiences around the world. He is passionate about ministering biblical, compassionate truth to those dealing with a personal and often secret struggle with homosexuality. He shares his experience and expertise with audiences across the country and as a regular guest speaker at Focus on the Family's international conference on homosexuality, "Love Won Out." A popular author and media guest, Alan has been interviewed by the Associated Press, the *Los Angeles Times, The New York Times, Time* magazine, *Newsweek,* the Fox Network, and CNN. He and his wife, Leslie, make their home in Florida and are the proud parents of a son and daughter.

www.exodusinternational.org
www.alanchambers.org

Exodus International
P.O. Box 540119
Orlando, FL 32854

(407) 599-6872

Yvette Schneider, author of the chapter "When You're Leaving Lesbianism," is the director of Women's Ministry for Exodus International. Her life was radically transformed as a result of encountering Jesus Christ, who delivered her from lesbianism and occult involvement. Yvette was in college campus ministry for three years, then became a policy analyst with Family Research Council. Her primary emphases are understanding the roots and causes of gay and lesbian behavior, effectively reaching the gay community, transforming from homosexuality to mature Christianity through one-on-one discipleship, personal testimony, and understanding and achieving God's destiny. Yvette and her husband, Paul, are the parents of two daughters.

Mike Goeke is a counseling pastor at Stonegate Fellowship in Texas. He also directs Stonegate's Cross Power Ministries, which reaches out to married couples impacted by homosexuality and helps churches minister to people affected by homosexuality. He was executive vice president at Exodus International for two years and currently serves on its board of directors. Before entering ministry, Mike practiced law for several years. He holds degrees in finance and law from Baylor University and Texas Tech University. Mike and his wife and ministry partner, Stephanie, have three children.

More excellent Harvest House books on homosexuality

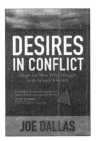

Desires in Conflict: Hope for Men Who Struggle with Sexual Identity

Joe Dallas

For more than a decade, *Desires in Conflict* has been the definitive "must read" for those who wonder *Can a homosexual change?* This book offers compelling reasons why the answer is yes.

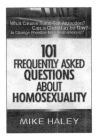

101 Frequently Asked Questions About Homosexuality

Mike Haley

Homosexuality has become acceptable in our culture. Homosexuals are adopting children, appearing as characters on television programs, and even seeking the right to "marry" their partners. Is this acceptance healthy for society?

Mike Haley, a former homosexual, answers the most often asked questions about homosexuality.

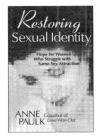

Restoring Sexual Identity: Hope for Women Who Struggle with Same-Sex Attraction

Anne Paulk

Restoring Sexual Identity offers answers to the most commonly asked questions by homosexuals desiring change and friends and relatives of women struggling with same-sex attraction.

The author draws from her own experience and that of many other former lesbians who participated in an extensive survey on same-sex attraction.

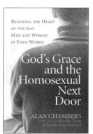

God's Grace and the Homosexual Next Door: Reaching the Heart of the Gay Men and Women in Your World

Alan Chambers & the Leadership Team at Exodus International

Author Alan Chambers—a former homosexual—and four of his colleagues at Exodus International offer practical and biblical insights on how both individuals and churches can become a haven for homosexuals seeking freedom from same-sex attraction.

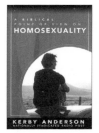

A Biblical Point of View on Homosexuality

Kerby Anderson

Homosexuality has moved from the margins of society to the mainstream. Christian apologist and radio host Kerby Anderson sorts through myths to deliver the facts on homosexuality and the social impact it has had on families, the church, schools, and traditional marriage. With a balance of God's truth found in the Bible and a desire to reach out to homosexuals, he answers key questions:

- What percentage of the population is homosexual?
- Did Jesus remove God's condemnation of homosexuality?
- Is there a connection between gay teens and suicide?

Anderson also looks at the spiritual aspects of homosexuality and offers practical suggestions for Christians reaching out to gays and lesbians.

To learn more about Harvest House books
and read sample chapters, go to:

www.HarvestHousePublishers.com

HARVEST HOUSE PUBLISHERS
EUGENE, OREGON